Standing on Bray Head
hoping it might be so

Colum Kenny

A Kestrel collection of poetry

First published 1995 by
Kestrel Books
48 Main Street,
Bray,
County Wicklow.

ISBN 1 900505 00 2.

Printed in Ireland by Falcon Print & Finish Limited
Bray, County Wicklow.

Facilis descensus Averno:
noctes atque dies patet atri ianua Ditis;
sed revocare gradum superasque evadere ad auras,
hoc opus, hic labor est.

It is easy to go down by Avernus:
night and day the door of dark Ditis is open;
but to return and to emerge where gentle breezes blow,
that is what must be done, and it is hard.

Virgil, *Aeneid,* vi, ll.126-29.

Contents

Early view of the Main Street, Bray, [*c.* 1880s].

(Lawrence collection, Cabinet no. 1866)

Note the sign above the entrance to Leverett & Fry
which reads, 'By appointment to the Royal Family'.

Compare this with the later view on p. 52 below. Among other
changes the first gaslamps, erected in 1860, and the unusual
building third from right, with an arched entrance, disappear.
An entrance to Florence Road will be made on the left.

A note about the illustrations

On the front cover is 'Bray Strand, Co. Wicklow', from a copy sketched and drawn on stone by T. Packer. This was first published by Bernard Wiseheart of 42 Lower Sackville Street, Dublin, before 1882. After 1885 the Martello tower was demolished in the process of erecting a cement wall and embankment as a new promenade and a defence against flooding.

The hand-coloured print from which this copy is made hangs in Bray Public Library. I am grateful to Bray Public Library for allowing me to reproduce it and to the library staff in general for their assistance in the preparation of this collection of poetry.

Included in the collection are many photographs of Bray from the William Lawrence collection. These are reproduced by permission of the National Library of Ireland. Most of the originals were taken over one hundred years ago and some are over one and a quarter centuries old.

The Lawrence plates are undated but Noel Kissane (*Photographs from the collections of the National Library of Ireland* (Dublin, 1990), page vii) states that some Lawrence photographs are as early as 1870.

It is reasonable to assume that Bray was visited early by Lawrence as the town was a popular seaside resort. The picture of the barque 'Thomas Ferguson' was taken before the harbour was built in the 1890s and, being a 'stereo' plate, may be as early as 1870. The shot of the International Hotel reproduced below looks no later than the 1880s, while one of Brabazon's Corner in the National Library shows the remains of the wooden viaduct which was disused following the rail crash of 1867. A number of Lawrence photographs show the full length of the new 'Grand Marine Promenade' which, as already noted, was only constructed from 1885. One Lawrence photograph, not reproduced here, shows a railway footbridge which was gone by 1895. In another shot, which is reproduced, Wyndham Park features. It was built about 1893. The western opening of Florence Road, visible in the later picture of the Main Street but not in the earlier one, is said to have been made about 1900. An estimated date is given below for each photograph.

Preface

Here you will find a poetry of the everyday. It does not strain for meaning and it does not purport to be perfect, either in its formal structure or in the unstructured view of reality which it reflects.

Old certainties have been fractured in the course of the twentieth century. Traditional explanations and systems of belief no longer provide the same shelter they once did.

In such circumstances there is a consolation in poetry. Through creating it and reading it we may continue to experience communion with one another and with whatever we feel transcends the individual. Poetry holds a door open, without requiring us to define what lies beyond.

I did not set out to write a collection of poetry. My original intention was to phrase my perceptions in prose. I was interested in finding a way of expressing my optimism in the possibilities of the future without resorting to posturing or to assertion. These poems suggested themselves to me.

Everyone finds their own way along the path on which they walk. Some convert an understandable feeling of alienation from their environment into the cult of isolation or obscurity. Alternatively, some seek to reconcile their consciousness with the cosmos in which they exist. There is a zen precept which seems to me to express the realisation of this less desolate option: 'Before enlightenment, cutting wood and drawing water. After enlightenment, cutting wood and drawing water'.

This author does not purport to be enlightened. There is no rounded view of the world advanced here. These poems are offered principally for entertainment and for enjoyment. I wish those who read them happiness.

i

Salad days

Wyndham Park, [*c.* 1895].

(Lawrence collection, Royal no. 1675)

Touched by beauty

The years slipped by
and they wondered
a usual wonder

where does time go?

as the two of them then
became the two of them now.

Touched by beauty,
their arms clutched handlebars,
not being so much at ease
as at attention,
all words and smiles to please
covering their nervousness.
Her soft skin and his brave voice:
Meet me against the future
and I will hold you close.
Before winter came
warmth blossomed
in a quiet sort of way
and they cycled their roads,
not yet ready
for something more intense.
The open air and sun
nurtured a growth
and the rest is easily told
although it took two lifetimes.
They laboured, learnt and loved,
kissed, married and had children.
Troubles came and went
but they hung on
enjoying ample fortune.
They sidestepped tragedy
tending their garden gratefully
and when it came to Christmas
bought bicycles for their boys.
It is not always so
around the bend
or down the road
and even when it is
it never lasts for long
except in photographs.

Brush

She recalls
feet brushing treetops and the thrill
that she might fall into the void,
her brother's arm around her.

To heady heights the old chairs cranked away,
now rotting metal stands where once she rose.
'They should have kept it going' and the rest
day-trippers landing in an eagle's nest.

Riding high

O George
what a magnificent world
stretching out on every side
such possibilities ahead of you
standing beside Black Tom
the Irish brought to heel
and strong government in its seat
England at the centre of it all
your brand new chambers
erecting
at King's Inns
by the River Liffey

Sauntering
across the inns piazza
master of those vital rolls
mounting your carriage
one fine evening
passing through walled Dublin
intent for Wicklow
and your well-stocked deerpark
by the Glen of the Downs
no matter who resented you
yours was the future
then

No time to consider
the herbs of summer
trampled underfoot.

Why not Bray?

'But if it is merely a matter of getting me out of the way', said Neary, 'while you work up Miss Counihan, why need I go to London? Why not Bray?'

It's Bray!
Yes, Bree or Brea!
The sea! A noble sea!
Beautiful view all bare and glitter,
a pleasing sight of sweeping bay to Dalkey or to Howth.
Let's say they called it Bray because it made the heart happy.

Brea
rang a bell
and resonated.
It sounded as it should.
So when they buried a great man
they raised up stones to make a kingly hill
and those who braved the windy pass knew Dún Brea.

By Jove! Dar bríce!
Red river ran full with trout
and kin of Britons praised Brighid
by the banks of bubbling Bray water.

Welcome those trout
as source of sustenance
for weary warriors Uí Briúin,
the O'Briens fleeing from the west
who found a refuge in Uí Briúin Cualann
and stayed to make this place of Bree their own.

Normans came later,
up from a river crossing
they climbed to build castles
and along the hill, or 'brí', grew Bree,
this town spreading outwards and onwards
to where the head of Bray Head stretches its neck.

We are alive in Bray
a place of such presences,
let us make of it what we will.

Them and us

 'What! You are giving up your queen? Sheer madness!'

Although
it's a pleasure
to drop a letter
through the slot
of those pillar-boxes,
once red but now green,
bearing your monogramme,
I cannot imagine how I might
have thought you my queen ever.
H.R.H. of Romania attracts me more,
jaunting about Kilruddery, than does VR.

I try to picture myself,
walking on the Esplanade
one summer evening in 1890,
the band playing upon its stand
'God Save Our Gracious Queen'.
'Our' queen?

It was always 'ours' and 'theirs', 'them' and 'us'
and those who stood in the middle got their heads rapped.

They who thought her theirs
to honour their gracious queen
erected an obelisk on Bray Head.
They who thought her definitely not
blew it away with dynamite.

Their queen reigned over a system
which denied home rule
and parity of esteem
to us.
Backed by their army
and their jobbery
they were satisfied

and we shared in the spoils of a greater empire
but it was never enough.

Them and us divided Ireland.

7

Picnic at Redford Cemetery

Early one New Hampshire morning
when I was young and walking out the road
taking the air and visiting town before work began
I passed the cemetery at Portsmouth
and breathed the smell of death
and it was sickly sweet
and silent.

and any morning afterwards
if I found myself that way
my nostrils flared and
my stomach rose
in excitement.

I was not one whom death had visited
no orphan boy nor child of widower
both war and disease rode past
me and mine.

Jaunty and green as summer in New England
my body warming with the risen sun
that mist exuded by the corpses
assuaged my romantic thirst
and I drank of life.

Standing on Bray Head I can see Shanganagh
where my buffeted father lies alone
the lines of departed deposited
near Woodbrook golf-course
where he once played.

Michael B. Kenny died when I was forty-one
and bending over his body on the bed
I kissed his still round forehead
cold and smooth as marble
and silent as a grave.

And I knew that we could never speak again
the distances would always be distances
as they are between the living
and I wondered for whom
I cried then.

It seemed in the weeks after my father died
that he had been left alone on shore
and I watched the land receding
as once on a beach at Skerries
I had been left behind.

Way out in the wilds on the side of the head
in the too small cemetery at Redford
with the company of headstones
a man takes the air willingly
and laughs.

He lunches lightly by his father's gravestone
knee-deep in long weeds engaged in
scrutinising droll inscriptions
and sitting on a tomb eats
bread and a banana.

Waiting for God, o to go on we can and must,
wander among these toes turned up
give consolation by example
rejoice in loving memory
and what may be.

Inconspicuous grave against a whirling wind
where by the sea father lies buried
victim of love and reparation
works and suffering over
o sacred heart.

Gas 1974

I spoke to a stranger
in New York
and he led me on
through Manhattan.
We met at the Met
introducing ourselves
by an Edward Hopper
I soon forgot his name
but not the way that day
and then again the next
he took me out to
interstices
in the crystal of his town
along the avenues
we walked for miles
where every building
held more than one story
into the Bowery
to a place down and outs
were fed a meal
and had a chance to rest.
That sallow man in overalls
a catholic worker
by Wyeth and Picasso
stepping his thin step
swopping old jokes
and dreams
and after a final
french fries and coke
bidding farewell
above a subway stairs.

ii

September breeze

Regatta Day, Naylor's Cove, [*c.* 1895].

(Lawrence collection, Royal no. 11366)

Standing on Bray Head

Standing on Bray Head
up where
a strong wind off the sea
blows green
the peat and gorse
from cross to marker
breathing space.

How I climbed here
along the permanent way
and where
I am to go
by some concealed footpath
are questions
blasted by the breeze.

A man of certain years
no longer young
I am
considered middle aged
although my end's unknown
rambling
on this deserted headland.

Here is a fool
who dares
to talk
maddened by madness
and the certainty
of fools
my chest finds voice.

As early in Athens
one summer Saturday
mounting the hill
I found
past tourist stalls
a quiet corner
of the Acropolis.

Hot
above the pollution
and cluttered concrete
of that too modern city
I rested silent
and heard an ancient voice
rustle the long dry grass.

My friend a Greek
filming
to alert the world
was hoisted
onto the pediments
of the Parthenon
and broke down in tears.

I have climbed
along these knolls
of Bray
and heard a whisper
calling
out of
Ballynamuddagh.

Townland of the poor
close to the earth
and closer too
its heaven
which I assail
in expectation
now.

If in
this generous sweep
of sky and sea and land
nothing exists
beyond what seems to be
then what remains
is inconceivable.

Here on Bray Head
over a misty sea
I chant an 'Om'
which rides the wind
in tune
like the sweet stick
on a Donegal fiddle.

'Om mani padme hum'
I sing
where none can hear:
turning to where a cross
invites
a Christian syllable
I try the name of God.

God
is a word
become so loaded
with the crust of theory
and the weight of hierarchy
it falls like lead
upon the mica-schist.

The wind roars
in my head
clutching my cap
I feel a sound rise
right
it is the Irish
Dia.

Dia duit,
agus dóchas freisin.

Bray water

The swans each year
find refuge
treading Bray water

At the river's mouth
snow white
gracing the harbour

Melancholy harbour
half-hearted,
ill-begotten, project

Block of breakwater
never right
scorned by high sea

Down from Glencree
this water
carried silting sands

Days of coal or wood
busy days
short-lived and gone

And lighthouse sank
fell slowly
underneath the tide

The fishermen's nets
hung bare
beside their cottages

Then lanes or homes
now space
to park sailing boats

The swans each year
find refuge
treading Bray water

At the river's mouth
snow white
gracing the harbour.

Unique I

The sun has crossed a golden bridge to me

alone

I stand against the cliffs and cloud-dashed sparkling sky

and only I

can see from where I see what I see now.

So fresh a morning this
after the stormy night before.

The world dissolves
lightening my heart and soul

A dazzling dance shines across a surging sea
from Greystones harbour to the lighthouse of Bailey.

Unique III

Along the path
the solitary wind-swept path
I have greeted the clear morning briskly
facing ahead beyond a long and muddy stretch a turn
which being reached will be a little nearer my own end
and glancing round as though I was approached behind
I thought I caught a glimpse of how I'd come this way
then turning forward again and shaking my head clear
it seemed a transparent image of myself walking on
for one split second framed in time
in watery sunlight me three
along the path.

Suburban litany

There is a contempt
in the contemplation of
formless suburban housing estates
sprawling around Bray and other towns.

There are emotions
held in reserve and
directed by those who don't
against those who do
dwell in such suburbia:
against a mass dismissed as
cautious, penny-penching and predictable,
varieties of privet hedge and baked beans,
in a land of breakfast cereals,
child-minding and the school lunch,
non-stop TV and mid-range cars,
and clothes from Dunnes and Roches,
or Marks and Spencers,
and fear and mortgages
and going to church from habit,
a people not at all accepted as
the discerning, classy, sensitive,
emancipated, free sort
the others are.

This is how we try to separate the chaff from wheat.

You strike a pose and hang on for dear life.

But

In Ardmore, we aspire.
In Ashton Wood, we anger.
In Ballywaltrim, we believe.
In Charnwood, we care.
In Clover Hill, we carp.
In Corke Abbey, we cope.
In Elgin Heights, we eat.
In Fairy Hill, we fight.
In Glencourt, we greet.
In Glencullen, we grow
In Herbert Park, we hate.

In Kilbride Grove, we give.
In Killarney Heights, we kiss.
In King Edward lawn, we love.
In Oldcourt, we oppose.
In Richmond Park, we rage.
In Rosslyn Court, we reflect.
In Ryecroft, we read.
In Seacrest, we suppose.
In Silverpine, we sleep.
In Violet Hill, we vie.
In Woodbrook Lawn, we laugh.
In Woodbrook Glen, we weep.

And in Wheatfield, we chafe

at those who suppose
that they are superior
because they do not live
where we live,
who when the chips are down
will soon be seen
for what they are,
our flesh and blood,
consoling themselves
in flats,
in ideal homes,
in period terraces,
or detached houses,
in envy or
disdain,
inherited wealth or
an inherited attitude.

Another mountain

'A stunning motif', as seen from a train,
you wrote to Zola:
as when it swan into my view one day
seen from a road,
a shimmer of summer rock and shrubs.

Again and again you attempted to paint
Mont Sainte Victoire:
master of the plain by Aix-en-Provence
on 22 October 1906
you fell dead sketching it in a rainstorm.

This seemed an impression of the artist
at one with his task:
showing the world the endless forms of
Mont Sainte Victoire
you heartened me exploring Bray Head.

My imagination saw your bathers strip
at Naylor's Cove,
dreamt Bay of Marseille from L'Estague
like Killiney Bay
and met a kindred pine tree on a slope.

But, fellow law student, so obsessed by
Mont Sainte Victoire,
was what you tried so hard to capture
Louis-Auguste Cézanne,
dominant, bourgeois, self-made father?

Poetic, fantastic, jovial, erotic, physical,
geometric Paul Cézanne,
withdrawn to circle and to encompass
in Mont Sainte Victoire
total knowledge of nature as notation.

Seeking essential forms or cubic order
in Mont Sainte Victoire,
the genius of your art celebrating life
under the Chateau Noir
transcending your quest for certainty.

iii

Leaves of autumn

Bray Esplanade, looking north, [*c.* 1886].

(Lawrence collection, Royal no. 1673).

Leaf

Girl with a late blown leaf
caught in your lovely
long black locks
this early morning,
why do you turn and grab
angry as storm
goosed by a hair-tangled withered scrap?
As if trapped in a web of weather
you fly to fear
hand plucking to get it off
and then rush on exasperated
to catch the seven fifty eight from Bray.

Smoke

brown and blackened roots
where smoke drifts east
a headland slowly burning
above the boys and girls
at seven-a-side

dull thud
of leather boot against a ball
and
silent billowing plume
a calm foreboding

here is the omen of
winter coming
the sea laid low
still and smooth
as a blade
set to cut

across the spread of water
like the spires of a cathedral
viewed from the plains of France
two chimneys rise
the power of Pigeon House against the night

Par-3

Beneath a tossed and bright October sky
the yellow-rusted leaves freefall and lie

Sun draws the evening off a well-mown hill
and waves below move steadily to the beach

Calm heart and shadows on the cropped grass
and spring of turf pressed by the slanting light

The sea runs on as I am three waves older
and on the hill the shadows stretch and grow

This urban golf-course is deserted now.
its greens and tees etched out along its slope

Against the evening sky two silhouettes appear
bowing and swinging on a stage of levelled green

Rushing down emerald dunes they scamper off
above the sea young golfers go home from Par-3

The hotel lounge

Indifferent food.
Indifferent faces.
Outside it lashes rain.
In here the air is thick
and at the tables
draped in shrouds
the people eat
as if it were a chore.

Is this how I look too?
Perched on a bar stool,
jerking limbs,
glancing at my watch,
bitching about the toasted sandwich
and the service,
the grudging, almost efficient,
service without a smile.

Conceal not the blood

On shifting ground
turbid by nature and remote
a blood-thumping pulse upright
footstepping stones laid down
beneath a cold and swirling sea
and folded over
by furious magma thrust
the granite sparkling
glacier cooled
glacial drop
weathered
upon this rock
and sub-atomic void
in any tongue
in long-lost tongue
without tongue our land
and all that remains
what we were then
the bones of a goshawk
on Dalkey Island
six hundred million years had passed
before the falconer let fly
above some hunter-gatherers
six thousand years ago
in mesolithic time
and later in neolithic prayer
we gathered at a cairn
behind Bray Head.
a thousand years
and then a thousand more
we are
the Celts
conquerors come
who told tall tales
and fought like maddened dogs
to hasten death by glorious gore
as carnage was visited on
the plain below by
Builg sallying ashore
living within the raths
the septs of Cualu:
men, women, children
thinking, cooking, loving,
lying, stealing, cheating,

murdering, creating,
our tongues wagged
in an archaic sound
and all the while
a steady tide
submerged this coast
we are
Roman sailors
come
to make
girls pregnant
and we are
Roman missionaries
impregnating minds
with ancient tales
recut to measure
we are
Dál Messin Corb
Uí Dúnlainge and Uí Máil
slaughtered as a quern crushes corn
Uí Théig put to the sword
by conquering Uí Briúins
in mortal combat
and we are those who
while on that noble sea
thrilling under a full sail
bear down from Denmark
to plunder Glendalough
and lay waste on every side
until we tire of too much tide
and settle from Stagonil
to Ballygunner and Curtlestown
and growing soft with age
we fall under a Gaelic whirlwind
and this is but one thousand years ago
so that high up along the head
walking the lonely path
it is not hard to see
out of the middle-distance come
MacGiollamocholmógs
with shields and tunic
going to Raheenaclig
to thank their God
and God was on our side again
coming from Wales
with native allies

taking Dublin
and killing the primitives
who would not bend their knee
to Walter de Ridelesford
our noble baron of war
friend of Strongbow
Richard deClare gave him Bray as his own
And to Maurice Fitzgerald
si li donat wikinlo
entre bree e arklo
co fud la tere de kylmantan
entre ad cleth e lochgarman
in any tongue
Uí Briúin Cualann
under motte and bailey
and Norman military might
but spared bloodshed when
Domnall Mac Giollamocholmóg
cut an inglorious deal
but not for long
O'Byrnes and O'Tooles
devastating the manor
burning Bray castles
on raiding forays
we are
Archbold and Lawless
scarred by rebellion
and by Black Death
we are
the town and mountain men
who left the fields of Bray
sprinkled with red corpses
one day in 1402 when
Bloody Bank was named
becoming more Irish
as we built our settlements
making a church for wanderers
where once a cairn was raised
we are
the Tudor autocrats
routing wild Irish
as we are
the goslings left behind
we are
the tired old English
too used to life to fight

new English iron
and people from the north
cursed by Cromwell
we are
and soldiers of King James
sleeping at Puck Castle
our monarch about to flee
abandoned to our fate
angry and vengeful
we are the papists
who praised God secretly
upon Bray Head
and starving and beaten
survived to die
in famine
and Huguenots
who fled intolerance
and landed gentry
and decent protestants
and rising catholic middle-class
and poppies on the fields of France
and fiery gunmen spitting blood
and burning barracks
and brother chasing brother
through the mill wood
The Civil War
we are
and orange bigot
and triumphant church
and narrow nationalists
we are.
those who lived
while others died
in Hitler's holocaust
and we stayed neutral
we are
the Dart decanted
Dublin blow-ins
and the unemployed
the traveller hated
and the gombeen man
the woman beaten
and the boys in green
and child abused
in past in present and in future
alien people amongst the Leinstermen

Home run

hitting sixty-five
and accelerating
encased in metal

a pure silver sky
black velvet hills
night yet to settle

overtaking a bus
willing its driver
look to her right

every leaf-bared
its detail distinct
against late light

following in lane
tail-lights ahead
after day's work

wood drifting by
mountainy slope
rears up in dark

on Bray by-pass
my home stretch
radio in each car

silhouette house
window glowing
a beckoning star

iv

Samhain

(1 November)

Martello Terrace, [*c.* 1886].

(Lawrence collection, Cabinet no. 1858).

Note the absence of a veranda.

James Joyce lived in the last house on the right.

Bray opera house

Sing

above the crying poverty of Little Bray

Strain

by a big house free from rot and damp

Soar

over the hunger and the chronic shame

Sweeten

to Nellie Melba and the Quinlan Operas.

Echoes

of James Joyce in the Boat Club concert

Effort

of Cyril Cusack playing in a pantomime

Elegy

as losing sight a conductor struggles on

Error

to mock music sung to uplift or delight.

Wolves

There are no wolves in Wicklow anymore,
that was so very long ago and they are gone.

Over the head a seabreeze blows and lifts
the rotten chairs slung from a rusted pulley.

Once, it is true, these hills were forested
and in the oak woods such howls were heard.

But none has prowled here for centuries
and children may presume that they are safe.

Down in the bushes the rustling sounds
of skulking figure moving with bathed breath.

In the thick royal woods wolves chased
and ran amok when famine stalked the land.

Waiting and watching her he scratched
and ruminated, licking lips wet expectantly.

The gentle wind lifted her pretty frock,
as young girl laughing to the breeze rose up.

Off the walls

Bray urban district councillors, at least four,
and the artists of their town
mingling at an exhibition
sipping wine and swopping pleasantries,
afraid to show their weakness or their ignorance.
Outside a gale blows.
Inside the guests sip civil wine
and mix with friends or strangers
seeking consolation for uncertainty.
'It's interesting'. 'It's very nice'.
Very nice?
That sweet-faced woman turns her head away and
waits for fruit forbidden.
That youth's being forced into a world he does not know,
a glee club full of hokey pokey men.
It's off the wall.
It's in your face the pleasure and the hinted pain,
the faith, the hope and equinox come round again.
Outside a gale blows
and rain sweeps down along the river.
Inside the old court house
a heritage dug from Spanish roots
and shipped to Ireland in Dutch wood
is reborn now for Wicklow with new blood.

Waiting at Clarke Station, Dundalk

for Sonja Kenny

Then the pipe played 'After the Ball was over'
to twenty ageing people in that waiting room,
who patiently resigned themselves to thought
of the day to come in Dublin and of days past.
And after that song it played a soothing waltz
for those twenty waiting for the ten-eighteen.
Not one of them was under forty years of age,
with glasses, greyhairs, wrinkles or a paunch.
Each one alone, where some had entered pair,
resting sedately on a varnished wooden chair,
or leaning against the neatly wainscotted wall.
There the railway memorabilia, in old frames,
faded in flickering shadow in an old ballroom.
For the pipe had summoned memories in each,
tunes sparking thought as eloquent as speech.
Then when the music ended and a silence fell,
it wasn't broken by unseemly sound or voice.
Come dancing ghosts in chamber of the G.N.R.,
who glimmer faintly on a shiney vacant floor,
old diamonds of brown and nicotine linoleum!
I see my mother walking toward a dance floor years ago:
smiling and light, she waltzes on my proud father's arm,
in open and bright release from worry and from worries.
But then again she's stepping toward another dance floor.
My niece is 21, partying at Kelly's up on the Vevay Road,
her grandfather gone to God, her grandmother now alone
and seventy-five and musing how life's too quickly lived.
Should I have taken her by the hand to waltz once more?
Knowing she might never dance again my heart cries out.
All moments pass. The pipe pipes new refrain.
A bevelled mirror over tiled fireplace reflects
light that is filtered through the frosted glass.
Portholes high in the entrance doors are clear,
revealing a bright blue sky of late November.
We feel vibrations of the Belfast-Dublin train,
'Been like a doctor's surgery' a woman cracks,.
yet no one laughs, still nursing an old refrain,
or talks too much when looking up the tracks.

Cosy

Now it pours
and it really pours
that lovely sound
when you are in and warm
and wind blows rain against the window
to complement the downpour in the drains
and it grows dusk
slowly dark as lights come on
and you are safe for now.

A bad enough parent

Help me, my sons.
I'm not sure how to father.
I never went this way before.
Am I too cloying or too harsh,
too little caring or too much the patriarch?

You tell us Dad. You were our age once too,
we got our lives from Mammy and from you.
Please just get on and do what you can do.

Forehead to wave

Howth Head, completing curve of Dublin Bay,
A granite terminus of DART trains from Bray.
Slumbering beast broaches both sea and sky,
Tethered to city lest this rocky pig might fly.
Along the flanks electric lights of bungalows,
And on its back gorse and wild grasses grow.

The dread

Leaves scattered
and huddled in drifts:
decay be still
while children kick over the traces.

Chill scent of late autumn
and the witches riding high:
in our heads 'what if'
the masks might slip.

What we thought
we stood for:
we clung to
what we thought.

Every tree stripped bare
branches awry straddled by wind:
And the howl of hot laughter in a crowded pub
Sipping consolation from the beer ads.

O the trick and treat of television
dreams the good people brew:
and that welcoming smile of
lighted pumpkins in the window.

There is a chapel in a town in Portugal,
macabre walls piled high with bones and skulls:
Heap without hope:
Hope?

Hope.
Hop, skip and jump and fly till dawn
lest we descend into an everlasting hell:
Pray that the gates may not prevail against us.

Hallowe'en night

Darkness seeps slowly but surely
over the bushes and hollows of this hill.
and down along a well-marked coastal road
some sense of purpose grips the car headlights.

Howth to Kish and back again
warnings of peril facing travellers
flash for those who stand on watch as
over the horizon a boat flickers into oblivion.

The shadow of night gathers
and flights drop across the bay
tail-light of each airliner's broom
beckoning across the blackened sea.

Build a bonfire
hide behind masks
play fearless at a party
and hope for the sun-rise.

Critics

I hear the voice of critics,
'total indulgence':
the critic who is me,
'just so much verbal diarrhoea,
vain, immature and stylised'
(whatever that means):
the critic who is she,
'unstructured, random thoughts,
suburban James Joyce, ersatz Samuel Beckett':
imitation intimation,
'such boring poems and penny-dreadful lines':
the critic who is you,
the critic who is he:
hurry now to find the words,
to catch them as they go:
the critics who are they?

Nuit Saint George

There is a lighthouse by the River Seine,
where the lamp of knowledge burns at night:
and ship-wrecked writers clamber through its door,
lashed by the storms of time and seeking ease.

Here is a beach where James Joyce landed safe,
and Henry Miller calmed his troubled soul:
its company welcoming each waif
who may, unknown, be an angel in disguise.

Like tumbleweed they blow along the quays,
to where George sits at zero altitude:
an ageing friend of Sylvia, gone to rest,
he mans this lighthouse as he manned her past.

And all around rise high the piles of books,
each volume stamped as it departs the shop:
those bought by customers being marked to show
that once they'd been received at *Shakespeare & Co.*

Late on a Sunday a pushed door opens wide,
I'd thought to browse at half-past ten at night:
within sits one who take a turn to watch,
bidding me bide my time as he writes prose.

In the 'poets' nest' a woman smiles on verse,
and I root out a Garland Joyce to go:
wishing 'God speed' to every vagrant Ulysses,
who may find here a respite from his wandering.

v

Paris

Quinsborough Road, [*c.* 1886].

(Lawrence collection, Royal no. 4788)

Looking east from Herbert Road across the Main Street.

Irish breakfast

The murmur of a Bray Cab at my door,
it's six a.m. and I'm still in a trance.
Out on the by-pass, in through empty streets,
to Dublin airport and a flight to France.

'May all beings have happiness',
as the plane takes off.
A sense of purpose grips me when I fly,
nearer to God and stretched across the sky.

Above Bray Head I sit back in my seat,
reading the news as we gain altitude.
Rising and bumping 'til we find our height,
an Irish breakfast as we meet the light.

The waves ran high when Wild Geese flew this way,
travelling from Ireland took time and trouble then.
Now, with my coffee drunk and papers read,
I land at Charles deGaulle in one hour ten.

Kill the machine

'Kill the machine',
someone had written
in a black felt-tipped pen,
on the wall by the steps
that lead down to the Seine.

'Kill the machine',
while electrons of traffic
discharged along the quay,
in English they inscribed
their small and transient plea.

'Kill the machine',
the tour tannoys squawk
on white barges in the night,
Notre Dame is dwarfed
by their shadows of arc light.

'Kill the machine',
here are replicas of stick,
thin plastic brooms of green,
being issued by the city
to keep the walks of Paris clean.

'Kill the machine',
police go on the prowl
moving in force of five,
stern faces and long batons
in their shadow hatred thrives.

'Kill the machine'.
Along this river walk
old doors are now filled in,
but new ways are needed
to help the poor and wavering.

Armistice Day

11 November 1994

Along the bustling Rue Saint André des Arts
embracing fate I grasp white roses to my heart.
Borne on Aer Lingus wings she comes to me
and we shall spend a weekend spending love.

That love is a kind of death it has been said,
but surely not that kind of death which those
who drenched the fields of France knew very well,
a metaphor too far for those who bled and died.

Jo loved her young man many years ago,
but he fell victim to the gunners' fire in Greece.
She lived her life in acting out a part
she never would have played if they had wed.

The Armistice was late for her who knew before
from Belfast childhood how one suffers hate.
She met her later fate as best she could,
fell in and out of love but always yearned.

Her ring is worn proudly by my wife today,
a pure gold band and symbol of recurring hope.
Holding each other in each other's arms tonight,
I'll count my blessings as an Icarus in flight.

Eugenie Hotel

An early morning smell,
through lanes and streets
sickly sweet, seeps from the Seine,
on the Left Bank.

Returning to the small hotel,
where we've checked-in,
I view 'Black Woman Using Aerosol',
on the Left Bank.

If life is a bed of roses,
no roses ever smelt like this
which 'freshens' the air for tourists,
on the Left Bank.

If still the artists stink,
of existential sweat,
they may not fit in here, as once,
on the Left Bank.

Just off Place Saint Michel,
and down a little rue,
we got ourselves a small 'en suite',
on the Left Bank.

Where cable says what gives,
from Buffalo to Bangkok,
it's U.S. news round the clock,
on the Left Bank.

Then and now

One

then,
or so it seems,
the same trees growing
all around the Luxembourg.
the same guards, still in their Senate stalls.
the same child pushing out the same old boat,
and I am who I was when first I came here years ago.
That pond looks smaller now than how it was,
the gendarmes younger, are a little bored,
and round the Luxembourg,
some trees grow brittle,
or so it seems,
now.

Two

In 1981
they drove to Paris with no children.
In 1983
two came again with one.
In 1985
once more there was a single child.
But back again in 1992
brought three.

And climbing the Eiffel Tower
by elevator,
the family of five
lifted towards the sky.

In 1994
alone again in Paris
two lie in bed,
discussing children.

The garden flowers

for Sam

Three long neat sheds
of potted plants and cane
where people duck
to shelter from the rain.

Here orchids elegant,
there Bonzais trim,
and greenery profuse
as darkness closes in.

These garden flowers
pour Monsieur et Madame,
beauty in bloom
spread out near Notre Dame.

The day is fading,
light scents fill the air,
for balcony or vase,
they groom perfection here.

Confession

'Restaurateurs are like confessors',
she declares suddenly at dinner:
Gregory of Tours, forgive us our excess.
To please a body is to praise its Maker.

Les Trompettes De Versailles

'Work's out today'
pipe the bright and the good
heartening those downcast,
with their brass and their wood.

'Work's out today',
as two trumpeters flaunt,
by candle tonight,
in the fourth arrondissement,

'Work's out today',
as the organist plays
a factory siren echoed
by Monsieur Georges Bessonnet.

'Work's out today',
as we tap the stone floor,
in the incense and calm
of Saint Julien-the-Poor.

'Work's out today',
as for hundreds of years,
at this little church,
joy has rung in the ears.

Moths

So moths, like men,
cannot leave well enough alone.
Flying too close to flames,
they burn
or fling themselves to die on glass,
seeking the source of what is bright.
Even in vain tonight,
within this ancient church,
against an electronic spot which is turned off,
one beats in desperation
at reflected candlelight.
Yet on this holy ground a welcome may await
when such ones fall.
for God *is* Light
and in Him, it is written, is no darkness found at all.

Safe home

And then she's away,
down through the R.E.R.
and out over sea,
bright star of my night
shooting across England.
If she had never come
alone would not feel so.
We stand two in one,
lamps warming space
that much less clear
when Catherine's out.
Retracing our steps,
I turn on cobblestones
to ancient Saint Julien.
Long waxen candle lit
before icon of women,
a beacon as she flies,
making her way home
to where three gather
in our name.

One wind

It is one wind blowing
great-grandfather along Amiens Street
grandfather round the Praça do Comerçio
my father at business in Abbey Street
I crossing the Pont Neuf today
my son stepping out at Booterstown
making our way in the world
we are blown as the leaves
season upon season, age to age.

vi

Home for Christmas

Main Street, Bray, [*c.* 1900].

(Lawrence collection, Royal no. 1678)

Compare this with the earlier photograph
published as the frontispiece above.

Christmas on Bray Main Street

'The town has a cheerful and interesting appearance'

- Samuel Lewis, 1837

Up and down the busy main street see the people weave and wind
Under flickering Christmas lights a fair cross-section of human kind

Traffic jammed from bridge to town hall on *The Heritage Centre* side
Shoppers spending cash and credit, their plastic carriers bulging wide

In the card-shops business thriving *Occasions* has greetings and gifts
Such little novelties make presents to pick and choose as you think fit

Molloy's or *Dixon's* for fresh breads, cakes or puddings or mince pies
Sasha's for the well-dressed woman or *Allen's* for men's suits and ties

The murmur of some pub for one drink, maybe a Ballygowan or tea,
A pint of Guinness with some friends and warm aromatic Irish Coffee

Outside in a glistening darkness street-traders manage as they may
Under tinsel and rain and glare selling gift-wrap or sketches of Bray

By the doors of *The Brew* a drunk, rough and tough and headstrong,
Confronted by two young Gardaí who red-faced tell him 'move along'

Lines of people in the pound shops, blocking aisles they push or grab
Japanese and Chinese knick-knacks or tinted sweets with 'E's and flab

In pride of place on the main street *Dubray's* bookshop painted blue
Where Mrs Clear attends the bridge steering her passengers and crew

Breathe in the smell of new books piled on tables enticing to be held
And fingered open by the curious for whom a forrest has been felled

Busy counters in the lending houses, *Bank of Ireland*, *Ulster* or *AIB*,
Trustee Savings Bank is dealing where *Mullen Brothers* once sold tea

Canopied butcher's shining counter, fresh turkeys at so much pound
Ham on hooks and blocks at *Doyle's*, sawdust strewn on tiled ground.

Warm *Caprani's* for the best of pork and bacon smells from childhood
Spiced sausages, back rashers or big black puddings made with blood

Sub-post office green and quiet, pensions paid, parcels sent air-mail
On-line for lottery and welfare, in its old shop-front are toys for sale

53

Bouquets or a wreath from *Ryan's*, flowers gift-wrapped are nice
And at the *Town Hall Bookshop* find novels and history at half-price

'Chick' Regan, wizard with words, in the place of his old mother goes
Dealing in birds and fuel or dreaming wild fantasies of urban heroes

Anvils and *Marks* must cope with volume discounts or some special
The super stores' bulk promotions threatening older shops' survival

By the *Village Gate Arcade* to parked cars, drivers getting mistletoe,
And busy newsagents are selling *The Bray People*, treats and tobacco

The chemist's cluttered shelves soothe desire, diseases or frustration
Pills, perfumes or protection at *Kennedy, Burke* or *Vance and Wilson*

Among the crowds along the footpaths mingle the 'idle' none employ
Threatened by bitterness who would be a 'Santa' for some girl or boy

Carol-singers lift their sweet sound but who raises a hardened heart
Not the band at *The Holy Redeemer* out of tune from the very start?

In the church pinprick lights with gold and white ribbon on the tree
Faithful between crib and cross at open confession or on their knees

Emigrants return or friends arrive to stay a while at *The Royal Hotel*
Eating their dinner and romancing where *Quin's* put up Dan O'Connell

Hits at *Golden Discs* of Garth Brooks, Daniel O'Donnell's tapes and CDs
No woman's hearts can resist as Christy sweats with The Cranberries

Video recorders at *Thorn/ E. M. I.* or a satellite dish from the *E. S. B.*
In *Fitzgibbon's* impulse buying a nice man's watch or some jewellery

Distracted parents pushing buggies by *H.J. Byrne* down past *Dunnes*
The cries and chatter of their children stirring memories in older ones

This festive time of loneliness a meal may keep heart and hope alive
Chinese celebrating Christmas in presidential birthplace (Number 85)

Where Murphy hid a TV camera racks of clothing wait pressed neat,
Each dry-cleaned garment for the big day in a *Marlowe's* plastic sheet

Single market

Is it not romantic
the Marienplatz market in Munich,
its December decked stalls
and mulled wine to ward off chills?

Isn't it traditional
the hawkers of Christmas baubles
girdled by quaint facades
redolent of times before the Nazis?

Isn't it impressive
that big clock with moving figures
and people stop each hour
expecting the bells to toll for them?

Isn't it very lively
the brassy sounds of a Tyrol band
rousing pedestrians' blood
in thigh-slapping memories of old?

Aren't they lovely
all the fine handmade decorations
frau selling me one recalls
a fancy golf tour to an Irish castle?

Isn't it so crowded
as Munich goes about its business
purchasing wooden angels
or gilt ornaments in this rich land?

Do jews still come
trading their wares in the market
or wondering 'never again'
when Germany dominates the E.U?

How did it happen
in this material and modern place,
are only buildings ersatz
and how many people really care?

The cattle

for Thomas Hardy (1840-1928)

Christmas Eve, and five of the clock.
Now they are all easily seated
Watching TV and waiting for 'Santa'
In a fantasy, centrally-heated.

Far from the madding crowd today
To the green headland I steal
Where high fields meet a pathway
That I might see cattle kneel.

Through mud amid primaeval rocks
Recalling the children I know
In the consuming commercial flood,
I'm still hoping it might be so.

Each family clustering round a tree
To view Nintendo, SKY or RTE,
While out on a fading wintery slope
I think of the coming century.

Christmas at Christ's church?

Why do we gather under different roofs
to celebrate?
Is God nearer in this church than in that
to celebrate?

In 1859 they stood on the Rock of Bray
to celebrate.
A church site from Lord Herbert of Lea
to celebrate.

Isn't it hard enough with all the anxiety
to celebrate?
Why set one faithful off against another
to celebrate?

Fr Healy had an act of disestablishment
to celebrate
William Gladstone helped peal the bells
to celebrate.

What on long scroll of church dishonour
to celebrate?
Catholic inquisitor and penal Protestant
to celebrate?

Buccini of Naples at The Holy Redeemer
to celebrate.
Salviatis of Venice rouses Christ Church
to celebrate.

Transubstantiation or consubstantiation
to celebrate?
Or the birth of Christ and Christmas joy
to celebrate?

Harmonium or Telford or Connacher set
to celebrate.
The organs in stained glass light playing
to celebrate.

On Bray rock how many churches stand
to celebrate?
To which would St Peter or St Fergal go
to celebrate?

By 1914 the RCs had their organ gallery
to celebrate.
By 1918 C of I choir had vestry's screen
to celebrate.

Did not great wars or nuclear terror join
to celebrate?
What is it that these churches call on us
to celebrate?

Voices of the children sing clear and full
to celebrate.
Mr Godfrey blesses each bosom heaving
to celebrate.

What did our early Methodist man come
to celebrate?
How Quaker found God in a turkish bath
to celebrate?

In 1940 RC PP and Presbyterian cut turf
to celebrate.
St Paul did not condemn joining together
to celebrate.

What of those who do not wish to come
to celebrate?
Or those who do not believe in any God
to celebrate?

Discouraged congregation meets by crib
to celebrate.
With Christmas tree and candle wanting
to celebrate.

Why does the baby's nativity give cause
to celebrate?
Did he also raise buildings and churches
to celebrate?

L'Irlandaise

Here he is running on the strand
on a mild Christmas day about 1890.
Jesuithastening from the political inferno
Jim and Stan leave Martello Terrace behind.
Packed off to Clongowes, when not even seven,
all for the greater glory of God to learn his letters.
Jim is now wandering with his brother by the grey sea
throwing stones or daring each breaking wave to wet him.
They turn to see Vance, the chemist, walking along the prom,
a cheerful man out for a good breath of ozone around the Head
where all the flies of Bray swarmed over Uncle William's new hat.

Here he is walking on the stones
one fine September morning in 1939.
About to hasten into the political inferno
Sam trods the rough and windy north beach
cooped up in his mother's house out at Redford
nerves jangling from the too small talk of relatives.
A young man with the itch to make and nothing to say,
the age of Jesus crucified, he turns his back on Greystones:
What doesn't face north faces east and he is the worse for it.
While he crosses under the crumbling cliff-path from Bray Head,
peering into a long black tunnel, Britain declares war on Germany.

But they met far from Bray Head
                    in Paris one evening in October1928
and Shem's Lucia, falling into the inferno,
                    sweet baffled dancer left her sanity behind.
Too sad Lucia wandering by Trieste and Zurich,
                    her heart burst opposite the Luxembourg Gardens,
recognising that Samuel desired her father but not her.
          Three great minds of the twentieth century drew a blank.
The words of Jung, Joyce and Beckett were of little use to her.
   Ah Lucia, where you are worth nothing you should want nothing.
Come dance on the headland, let bonfires melt away the malheurs.

Treachery

In memory of Jimmy Curran

There has come a time at the end of the year
when I rise early and set my face for Belfast,
driving hard to meet the primate of all Ireland.

Behind me deep in the hills sits Glendalough
once thriving centre of learning and industry,
courted by chieftains and famous for its saints.

Far from holiness this year the Irish church
racked by scandal and creaking at the joints,
all to its primate and cardinal a sorry trespass.

On a ledge above the deep lake Kevin slept
fasting and praying up to his waist in water,
stripped of comforts for the spirit's better care.

Now to this red-bricked bitter town I travel
and up the Ormeau Road seek out the house
where Cardinal Cahal Daly's sister lately dwelt.

Not all who followed Kevin were exemplary
and his monastic city had its fill of treachery
declining through strife to its most dismal state.

This Christmas Cahal Daly went home again
a pious old man wondering about the future
alone with family photographs but for his staff.

The spirit of St. Kevin was a great strength
through penal times when the Irish fought
to stay alive and remain sane in the onslaught.

The cardinal's thoughts recorded we lunch
his suspicions of the media allayed for now
canny prince of the church having done alright.

Dark day of mustard light and heavy rain
and filthy driving on the road past Newry,
who ravages and deserts your beloved church?

vii

Côte de misère

The barque 'Thomas Ferguson', [1870s].

(Lawrence collection, Stereo no. 1955)

At the mouth of the River Dargle,
before the harbour was built.
Note the beacon.

Ultra litora Iuverna

Not here. Not here.
Not here. Not now.
It is a mistake.
It was not meant to happen
like this.
Give us a chance
just one more chance
to see Rome
and to live a little longer.

Some say this bay is as beautiful
as that of Naples
but the weather is not so clement.

For seventeen hundred years
we will lie under Bray Head
waiting with Roman coins
to pay some ferryman
to take us over that
Stygian Irish Sea.

Maybe the phantom chief of the O'Byrnes
in a ghostly barque carried their spirits
to some distant shore
but he left the fare
with their remains
which looking solid
when at first exposed
vanished from sight in a few moments
crumbling into air and leaving only teeth.

So what is not visible now was once flesh and blood
Palladius and Patrick and their churchmen
and a pawn in the game of treachery
and merchant adventurers
and a papal bull
and imperium for a wayward people
more than one way to gain a foothold
or to plant the insignia.

To go to Rome

Again it has snowed
as it did then
when I first made it
into Tibet.

So many years since
I took a taxi
up out of Lockerbie
and to Tibet.

Slowly I was to see
that what is
may not seem to be
as in Tibet.

Who would believe
in Christ
that faith can lead
onto Tibet?

Two decades flew
as I fought
learning too little
about Tibet.

Rainbow or river
life passes
sit for a little bit
here in Tibet.

Dun Laoghaire/Holyhead   Holyhead/Dun Laoghaire

Swirling mid-winter passage
starboard the Kish sandbank
as Bray Head changes shape
relative to the Stena Sealink.

Captive to commerce aboard
passengers wander on decks
expected to maximise spend
and not to recall old wrecks.

Chattering monitors barrage
casual viewers with ad clips
corporate videos or features
ingested with plates of chips.

Video game or fruit machine
perhaps a drink or duty free
such spirit of free enterprise
amenities upon the Irish Sea.

Plastic confectionary of ferry
boat rigged as shopping mall
cinema to distract a seafarer
from pitch and toss of squall.

Out of a mist the South Stack
over murky depths of dread
down to car deck and fumes
a tomb opening to Holyhead.

Fort and island of Saint Cybi
where Romans kept a watch
a shelter to a hundred ships
when English ruled the Irish.

The drivers of cars or trucks
disgorged by a harbour shed
over Anglesey to motorways
and later rest in distant beds.

Upon my return to Holyhead
gales gust a cancelled sailing
but the B&I line does depart
into the wind's loud wailing.

Happy to be underway at all
grateful to avoid Welsh B&B
transferred to a lounge seat
on Stena's competitor at sea.

Rough going and rise and fall
soon breed a nervous silence
broken by sounds of retching
and purser's announcements.

Smack of waves on windows
heralds maritime technology
Danish to Dutch shipbuilders
jumbo *M.V. Isle of Innisfree.*

But into another deep trough
and shuddering bow to stern
shakes complacent voyagers
and whips up a real concern.

The Estonia was also modern
a towering Scandinavian ship
with hundreds of passengers
assuredly crossing the Baltic.

The car-deck door torn apart
a flooded ferry will list hard
to plunge fathom by fathom
joining *Leinster* or *Vanguard.*

Engines labouring four hours
sighting at last of Dublin Bay
no stall nor drift as *Leona* or
Lady Harriet to cliffs of Bray.

Annunciation

just an ordinary sort of sacred place

between Cable Rock and Greystones
a tree caught in the wind fluttering
its branches uttering a deep sound

a smooth January silver nakedness
surrounded by a white-flecked sky
and grounded on drenched grasses

a low, weak, dazzling southern sun
washes the breached lichened wall
as running water splashes my ears

no burning bush along muddy way
just a moment of calm expectation
when the blowing breeze subsides

and as I softly turn to face the sea
a bird of annunciation on the wing
swoops from the air and thrills me.

feeling good here

Windgates

for Oisín

and stop to look around.
below the survey marker
then reach a stony wall
of cattle dung and mud
plod through a minefield
climbing over two gates
passing the radio masts
up by the holly wood
to a cutting wind
our backs turned
we walk with

▲ *ASCENDING*

▼ *DESCENDING*

we walk then
by scorched land
on stalks of gorse
to join a beaten path
wheeling into the gale
sipping that snowy chill
of icy northern slopes
exposed before us past
Giltspur from Bray Head
blowing right through us
until we reach a shelter.

Up and away out over grey seas a man goes flying from Bray Head
a paraglider who'd never seen the winds behaving just like this
has taken his chances and with a grunt gone to join the gulls
which he had said were a sure sign of an easterly wind,
lifting out there and soaring without flapping wings.
He worried a while standing in gorse by the cross
arranging the yellow chute with orange stays
blue glow and purples of his gear shocking
winter wind shifting from north to east.
'You need at least ten miles per hour
or you go straight down', he said.
The chute gave out a 'whump!'
pulling him back and rising
as he swung into his seat
and fled at such speed
my heart leapt after
and he drifted on
over the boats

paragliding

Bonfires

It is
aflame!
Look up! Look up!
What largesse! What bounty!
The bonfires blazed on Bray Head then
and multitudes were fed by the lord of the manor
when Reginald, Lord Brabazon, married Mary Jane Maitland.
Who stood stoking the fires on that cold day in January 1868,
in organised joy that the conquering heroes were to multiply?
No spontaneous combustion then when Bray Head blazed in shame
one hundred and twenty Kilruddery workpeople being fed for free.
Each knew their place there, knowing that their place was not theirs.

It is
such details
of history that burn.
What largesse! What bounty!
The Brabazons, earls of Meath, gave gifts
returning part of the lands held for two centuries
Giving back a park and prom and building a Town Hall too.
But poor Reg had a dreadful time of it with the Land League
who told him to what best purpose a Town Hall should be put.
That noble Norman knight held out against contentious chatter.
He'd do no more for a Bray too vehement in religion and politics:
'So much for gratitude amongst the poor easily-led Irish', said Mary.

It is
their land
still here, Brabazon.
What largesse! What bounty!
These earls had not to flee from Ireland.
A street in Little Bray still bears a Maitland name.
When dying infants drove impoverished mothers to despair
men were despatched to light fires on Bray Head and feasted.
The wood glowed orange above and resentment burned below.
The earls of Meath built a fine house and gardens at Kilruddery,
defended king and another country, did charitable works, hunted,
farmed their land and dispatched the railway on its precarious way.

Bird in the bush

And as I turned away,
I heard a definite call.
Turning again I saw a
bullfinch on the gorse.
A mild and usual day
but only he at singing
and sitting on thicket.
Fresh the air whistled
as we essayed a duet
beyond the oak wood.
Stretching out a hand,
I though that stillness
might coax him to me.
It was no trifling bird
who turned and flew,
and left me reaching.

Ferns in winter

Anything more devastated
than tract of winter ferns?
See the mighty have fallen
and are laid waste around.
The firm gorse bush mocks
scattered twisted remnant
of once upright green fern,
withered and brittle thing,
sounding when seized dry
and crunching like distant
gravel, trod by a light foot,
brown body, beaten down,
recoiling from fierce blast
of wind or thoughts of ice.
Yet, what will green again
to live on hard headland?
Same fern? Seed of same?
Same difference in spring.

viii

Lá le Bríd

(1 February)

Quinsborough Road, [c.1886].

(Lawrence collection, Cabinet no. 1852)

Looking west towards Main Street.

Spring

yes O mount the hill of green wheat
shoots up muddy tractor track by wood
off royal road and climb again up wide
as water stretching field out towards the
summit and the slopes go on around and
past the wood and by the trees to please
yes please perceive the sprouting shoots
of cereal waving green and wavering hsh
hsh you can't ignore the droning traffic
but lost among the Wicklow sky and
clouds blown on and off the hills and
specks of snow to breath the cool air
mountainy dark with blue on green
fresh ground by a glorious sun o yes
please warm my face and tickle grass
that bending low young root of wheat
we eat and then the stupid sheep all
wool and baa come running up as if
to greet an old friend twenty three
all white and then one black too
who are disappointed as they
see that I am not he being me
and happy as a lark to sweep
on and up and over poxy rutted
track to crop of rock where gorse
pricks and I climb the maze to reach
a dead-end by the old farmhouse where
wind blows windmill and dark dogs bark
bold and then I turn and from that scene
I say o yes please more it's like a roller
-coaster can it last I fear it cannot that
one day soon they'll find this too and
then they'll come with JCBs and build.

9 February 1861

James Lacy was a brave man,
a braver man than me:
one day in a bold endeavour
he risked his life at sea

A brig was about to break up
in violent gales at Bray:
but Lacy with James Bowden
cheated death that day.

Ships went down at Wicklow,
the furious storm blew:
and five faced death at Bray
until that daring rescue.

Lacy and Bowden saved them,
taking aboard first four:
anxious to turn for land then,
yet there was one more.

If Lacy lashed him to himself
that man might survive:
so Lacy stepped into the sea
and both emerged alive.

Two fates entwined together,
by rope hauled ashore:
a monumental act of courage
entering into folklore.

James Lacy was a brave man.
a braver man than me:
one day in a bold endeavour
he risked his life at sea.

Glencree

Up near Lough Bray
on a desolate mountain side
a savage barracks soon abandoned
became a grimacing reformatory for boys.

Up near Lough Bray
knowing what we know now
we reflect on how power is abused
and grow uneasy in the shades of misery.

Up near Lough Bray
from the cottage in summer
with mother and brother you went
to attend mass at the reformatory chapel.

Up near Lough Bray
on that tribune young Oscár
you were kept apart from the boys
and their strong fresh threatening bodies.

Up near Lough Bray
you were baptised in Christ
wet-haired visitor to a remote gaol
safe with the chaplain and his holy order.

Up near Lough Bray
a mother not yet demeaned
by a husband's heterosexual excess:
it was a Brayman would foretell your fall.

Up near Lough Bray
in the glen of a shaking bog
where the Third Reich left its dead
and a statue in the woods is said to move.

Up near Lough Bray
in the old barracks and gaol
haunted by the spectre of violence
they have sought peace and reconciliation.

✠

Templecarrig

And was the glory worth it all?
It was a dreadful bloody business.
Let us surmise one truly noble knight
who went to war hearing of evil abroad,
outraged by stories of injustice and cruelty
and urged on by pope to join the great crusade,
only to find that rabble raised the cross of Christ
and madness seized the armies of European might,
sickened to his stomach by papal lies and bloodshed.

He withdrew with those who sought truth not terror
to search for mysteries in the temple of Jerusalem
and to be met in a secret brotherhood of knights.
But then one too long-awaited day he returned
riding along the soft, wet, coast of Wicklow
delighting in a family thought him dead.
Yet he felt a distance from his people,
so now on an ancient pile of rocks
he built himself a little temple.

Talking sense

Freshly baked loaf,
croissant and butter:
lifetime of pleasure
in a smell.

Sucking on aniseed balls
or sipping Ricard:
forty years of pleasure
in a taste.

Watching her colour rise
fire opal flashing:
twenty years of pleasure
in a sight.

Hearing a magic flute
music of Mozart:
ten years of pleasure
in a sound.

Feeling beneath her skin,
some kind of lump,
moment of terror,
in a touch.

Alarm-call

Quavering synthetic amplified bells
summon to church and scare the birds:
no gentle steady peal or bold clear clang
as once long gone sounded around the hillside.

And this is progress.

My telephone rings at midday:
Dick working Sunday in Manhattan
breaks from a chore to dream of Irish ease.
We gaze at our desktops and swop what's new.

He's been to Florida again to see his kids,
mine play upstairs or enjoy a football match.
I've been so busy since my wife was ill a month ago:
someone has dropped dead with whom he used to drink.

Over and out and hope to see you soon,
sounding a note that may perhaps ring true.

MUTOSCOPE

==

City lights/from up here on the hill/sterile lights/stretching out/
along/valley of diamonds/red river valley/and perching high/ on
Herbert Road/are Ardmore Studios/light into money/money into
light/eighty years Bray flickering/Willie Power/rolled a Gaumont/
all brass and shiny wood/who better to cry cut /when Rosaleen
pouted/Laurence Olivier out scouting/a long sunset/beyond the
meadows/ at Powerscourt/field of Agincourt/for Henry Five/ and
stars shine/Cagney and Mitchum/Wayne, Connery or Sheen/little
Mickey Rooney/and large Ustinov/Charlotte Rampling/ and Mel
Gibson/Tom Cruise and Nicole Kidman/and the rest/far and away/
a great little country/and tax haven/and best foot forward/for the

Oscars/of Josie MacAvin /and Brenda Fricker/and Michelle Burke/
and baby-faced Neil Jordan/our loving son in Hollywood/and
action on the streets/the Bray Post Office /a bureau of the US
mail/for a day/and snow on King Edward Road /in Summer/big
high dreams/ of the cast and crews/Bray tradesmen/and Bray
sparks/camerapersons/editors/pullers and grips/and other best
persons/in and out of work/and the patrons/glazed eyes
reflecting frames/going home in 1902/from McDermott's Picture
House/and later eating popcorn at the Casino/ or warming hands
in the back row/of the Roxy/or Panorama/and driving to Royal
screens/that modest multiplex /or renting videos from Xtravision.

==

Nowhere to run

When there is nowhere left to run?

with mountains dissolving to the sea,
hills overgrazed for E.U. ewe subsidy:
as for the Elizabethan crop of staves
stripped, so now by Brussels knaves.

When there is nowhere left to run?

each fall of rain washes off more soil
where greed and need led to despoil:
the forests destroyed exposing earth,
soft flows Italian and Himalayan dirt.

When there is nowhere left to run?

where clay dissolves cement sets up
apartments or buildings to 'develop',
and smother the spirit of each place
there had been wild or sacred space.

When there is nowhere left to run?

between the railway tracks and road
another house rises upon Bray Head:
again developers making their mark
between Rathdown and Raheen Park.

When there is nowhere left to run?

when mac Dunlaing beat Sigtryggar
Leinster victors turned to slaughter:
by Windgate site of that new house
from Delgany to Bray ran the Norse.

ix

March

Lower cliff-walk, Bray Head, [1870s].

(Lawrence collection, Stereo no. 2918)

Nugget

Stop
and listen,
you who shall be!
It is I, named Uchadan,
artificer of the people of Cuala,
smelting here gold for Tighearnmas.
There shall remain a lunula of Blessington,
kept in a London museum smelling of my sweat.
The marbles Elgin steals shall be much later fashioned.
Guarded together with such other booty I shall still impress,
and hearten hard-pressed artificers after thousands of years.

Song of the streets and of the woods

Victor Hugo remarked that,

'At a certain point in life,
if one is contemplating the future,
the inclination to look back
becomes irresistible.
Our adolescence,
that charming dead thing,
appears and demands consideration.
Moreover,
it is a serious and melancholy lesson
that in the same individual
two ages meet,
one beginning as the other ends.
It is useful
to confront the point of departure
with the point of arrival,
the fresh tumult of morning
with the calm of evening,
and illusion with conclusion.
The heart of man is a page,
on one side of which
is written *Youth*,
and on the other side of which
is written *Wisdom*.
Both sides of that page are found in this book.
Reality features in this book,
but it is a reality
modified by what in man
goes beyond the real.
This book has been written
after much dreaming, -
and a little recollection.
To dream is permitted to the vanquished;
to remember is permitted to the solitary'.

For my part,

I could not help it
considering the future
I had to search
and my past beckoned
inviting me to say
how I got here
appearing suddenly
it rose from the living dead
and engaged memory
like a grinning corpse.
We reach a point
upon some summit
betwixt and between
becoming and ending
one age gone
another on its way.
sometimes calm
maybe tumultuous
often confused
easily deluded.
Around the heart
is no clean sheet
but a crystal vase
dropped on a hard floor
youth and wisdom
caught in its flying fragments.
The borders of reality
run through this book
which has been written
where dreams meet memories.
The vanquished may dream;
the solitary must remember.

Time

Dawn once came
while I held Conor close:
and parting then
I left to spread the news.

The light of day
blue stunned a car-park
and startling ice
blocked our windscreen.

Time found out
in the moments of birth:
time finding us
in each instant of death.

Night fell at last
the day my father died:
and crying then
I fought to keep awake.

Hard letting go
as I dropped off asleep,
then wakening
I saw the world turned.

What a save!

for Conor

It's lonely work
being on that line
a ready goalkeeper.
quick enough to kick
or sliding through mud,
or diving or saving goals.
My son says he feels that
he is responsible for losing,
even when it's not his fault.

The intensity of effort is wonderful to watch when kids kit out
and pulling on team shirts in darkest red or burgundy gear up:
there's pushing and turning to distraction as they call or shout
scrambling for places on the team and running round non-stop

The excitement as boys and girls chase the ball to kick it hard!
blissfully booting or scrabbling until called to halt by a whistle:
then play begins in earnest, with its scuffle of no holds barred,
their opponents raking the field as a referee tries hard to cope.

Gone to a football fantasy of goals galore got in a blaze of glory
the cheerful children are oblivious to the manager's command:
bursting with energy to re-run from TV a famous soccer story
as parents and guardians strain and support from the sideline.

They trip along and swarm about in hope to strike a vital shot,
as Pat and George encourage effort and the passing of the ball:
delighted to score, but dampened when the others hit the spot,
at full-time tilting open and sweaty faces to guzzle their bottle.

The seal

Wobbly worried blobby baby
    blundering back to the water,
        what on earth possessed you
            to haul yourself up the beach?

Were you fleeing from danger
    only to find yourself exposed
        at the mercy of any stray dog
            on the sands of Naylor's Cove?

Did you want something friend
    human voice to tell us how it is
        to warn of Sellafield radiation
            or fish stocks ravaged by man?

Or were you seeking your own
    that little helpless one rescued
        who now finds safety enclosed
            and hand-fed at the Aquarium?

You turned on me doleful eyes
    terrified as I approached you.
        but I told softly of my concern
            while you pushed away in fits.

You covered the fifteen meters
    slowly pulling your body along
        on sharp rocks pausing for rest
            finally reaching the sea's edge.

Between the boulders you flee
    flicking your tail up in delight
        swimming out with confidence:
            go safely little grey-black seal!

Foundations

for Mary Robinson

You laid a foundation stone
when you came to the back of Bray Head
in the Spring, early in your presidency, on 14 March 1991.

On that stone rose a school
facing the headland and back to the wind
Saint Andrew's and Newcourt mixed sexes, sects and skills.

You laid a foundation stone
swearing your oath of presidential office.
a red rose surrounded by so many thorns at Dublin Castle.

On that stone you're proud
standing for the people you act their part
and bear the expectations of those who voted for changes.

You laid a foundation stone
praising that school, encouraging children,
where boy may sit with girl and able share with impaired.

Behind that stone Sir works
under the gaze of board of management
representing more churches than in Ireland usually unite.

You laid a foundation stone
a new inclusive Ireland may rise there,
people on mature reflection seeing a strength in diversity.

On a pedestal you perform
professional lawyer's eye to the future,
each patient smile and gracious word working for nations.

Crossing

for Marie Murphy

Alone
I stand on deck
north-western gales
whipping this ferry boat.

Now going home
as March day fades
I rise and fall
through moments of my life.

Around me run
the choppy turquoise waves
all silvery delicious
in the evening's wash.

Behind above the deep green coast
a full moon shines
in the clear sky
over Scotland.

Ahead beyond cold darkened cliffs
the late sun lies
on the grass
of Ulster.

Starboard out by the Scottish isles
low clouds muster
red and white
with snow.

My mind drifts
counting how often
I have sailed this sea
that wraps round Ireland.

For each of us
there always is
that final voyage
crossing a horizon.

x

Easter

Main Street from the Town Hall, [*c.* 1886].

(Lawrence collection, Cabinet no. 1845)

Note the Brabazon wyvern and troughs

The bridge over the Dargle

He is a lovely child
God bless him
in his little blue outfit
that Granny knit
wheeled over the bridge
all buggy, boots and plastic,
unable to breathe.

*

Laid off again
fuck it!
How much bad luck can one man have?
and Annie expecting again:
so much for condoms
got from a slot-machine
under the influence.

This fuckin hill
up over the river
with its fuckin bailiffs:
the rich have it their way,
firsₜ they catch fish
and then they
catch poachers.

The house is cold
and nothing cures Tom's asthma
and Mary cries too much
and Annie's brother
Jacko
is a lazy bollocks
and should go back to England.

This river keeps on going
and so do I:
but this is my last bet
it's time my boat came in
I'll gamble at the bookies
that poxy redundancy money.
What a joke!

*

I've crossed here everyday
eyes lifted to the hills
smelling that fresh clear water
praying to him
coming from church
alone
if there's a God why did Jim die?

Me and a warm car
stuck in this bloody traffic
right on the old bridge
popping the radio
feeling such energy
counting my money
counting the years.

*

Oh Jesus no!
not such a living hell
say it's a dream.
my mother will have a fit
I am so sorry
oh so so sorry late
that I am proof positive.

H.I.V.
like His Infernal Voice
(Shit! Here's old Maguire)
It was only the twice
(I don't want to talk)
and he seemed to be nice
('Hello Mr Maguire!')

Here by the old bridge
there in the water
that glint of glass
down there is lovely
where the river runs
water wash over
peacefully flow.

They'll think I slipped
over this parapet
too low for safety
they've said it for years,
Aids and the agony,
nothing to face now
but the last fall.

*

Bend over cold on granite
(and river in flood below)
to drift down dreams
of his warm muscled back
I want
the body and mind of him
who has a woman.

93

Easter Saturday

Cross without savour
its weight descends on me,
under a mass assurance
of victory for the Church:
too high, too hard, too big   (for Jesus?)
an ecstasy in engineering.
'Christo Regi, erected1950'
not 'Lamb of God',
suffered on Good Friday,
but 'Christ the King',
whose bishops rule, okay?

Too long chastised,
Irish catholics,
invited to erect
a more becoming symbol
than an obelisk to Victoria
or bonfires for Brabazons
got behind 'the first priest
born in the town of Wicklow
since the time of St. Patrick'
and raised this cross   (for Christ?)
in all its glory and its might.

Clambering up the hill
facing Martello Terrace
impressed by concrete
reinforced and reckoned
likely to last seventy years
above Quinn's farmhouse
where mass was celebrated
during penal years
a cross to teach love   (for others?)
Devil out of hell! We won!
We crushed him to death!

An barr buidhe

gorse may recover
although the land
is sorely scorched
deep rooted plant
watch bushes rise
slowly then spread
taking it softly
prickly resilient
the top of the hill
with gorse flowers
may be yellow again
better 'buí' as Gaeilge
buoyant and vibrant
buí, buí agus buíochas.

A bhonnáin bhuí, is é mo chrá do luí
is do chnámha críontar éis a gcreim.

Easter

A spring welled up,
so fresh the water ran
slaking his deepest thirst.
But high sea spray came on
And bitter salt filled the spring.

Then climbing up along the hill,
he yearned again for drink
to slake his deeper thirst:
Patrick bowing down,
a spring welled up.

The simple story of another age
for any who would live in hope,
quenches afresh the dry throat.

Where Patrick perhaps climbed,
they later built the little church
on ancient mound,- Raheenaclig.

Of stone and wood, now ruined,
surmounting an even older pile
its window to the morning sun.

Across its threshold to the sea
there stepped out once a friar,
who breathed deep a dawning air.

While all around grew old oaks,
echoing to the sound of its bell:
no town below then expanding.

Alleluia!

Sunday

The cliff opened up,
and out poured words
shaking the sure of mind.
Bedouin at Khirbet Qumran,
found Jesus wrapped in scrolls.

The first was fearful as he ran,
announcing his good news,
waking the pure of mind.
Muhammad adh-Dhib:
the cliff opened up.

Through Antioch and Jerusalem
news had spread to Alexandria:
there Patriarch preaches it yet.

In his orthodox church in Paris,
fourteen hundred years passed
before I stepped into its charm.

'Seigneur ayez pitié', as I stand,
enchanted by the ritual prayer,
and watch as time's doors part.

'Les portes! Les portes!', we cry
awakened by the peal of bells:
'En toute sagesse soyons attentifs'.

In French church styled Gothic,
and on Bray Head they prayed,
lest hope fade by the Dead Sea.

Alleluia!

The secret tunnel

It's said that an underground passageway
connects the old church and Smuggler's Cave,
but whether bad clambered up it, or good
dropped down, is something they cannot say.

That tunnel which somewhere lies hidden
is said to have helped the rebel Hugh Tallant,
when troops of the crown were after him,
raring to render their prey much less gallant.

A ship lay at anchor by Smuggler's Cave,
moored at the Brandy Hole under Bray Head.
and had Hugh not been guided in secret
then our hero might have sooner been dead.

But was there ever really a tunnel there,
where all of the granite and rocks lie so hard,
or had there once stood a passage grave
where that Rath of Raheenaclig is still bared?

Such grave would have faced to the sea
meeting the risen sun down a channel of gold.
People may have believed it the tunnel
where light greets dying spirits, so we're told.

Or the yarn of a tunnel may have shown
that sainthood and the state of sin are joined,
and people would have been reassured
hearing that tale by an old storyteller coined.

For there is always some secret tunnel,
as Sigmund Freud took pleasure in revealing,
and each person can find life's passage
disappearing through floor or through ceiling.

Says Con, 'We cannot lose our shadow!'
Doesn't my son put the truth fine and handy?
For a smuggler may make it to heaven
but the priest slip and drown in good brandy.

Yet this yin and yang may be fanciful
and the truth could be just what is written:
that a tunnel exists out on Bray Head
where both clergy and outlaws could fit in.

Prague spring

City of confusion and contradiction
cockpit of Europe and compromise!
Your darkest secrets lurk in alleys
as tours swell along thoroughfares.

Like greedy rats, from Stare Mesto
to Mala Strana now visitors swarm
past hucksters on the Karluv Most
feasting on a Baroque theme-park.

Praha takes advantage of invasion
as Hapsburg counter-reformation
or Nazi blitz or Russian occupation
brought suffering and opportunity.

A flexibility at Charles University
is disposed to embrace and resent
gold rushes of consultants itching
to exploit the new Czech Republic.

Standing in Staromestske namesti
Jan Hus affirms that 'Pravda vitezi'
(Kenny family says 'vincit veritas')
a promise that the 'truth prevails'.

But business prevails in this town
that martyr's legacy a work ethic
expressed in industrial revolution
flowering in the narodni obrozeni.

Czechs know how you turn a buck:
Skoda workers saluted gross Stalin
Duke Vaclav rushing to McDonald's
as radio bosses embraced Irish FM.

Past the taxis and decaying beauty
is that Praha Mozart already knew:
here people must make ends meet
and bend with the wind of history.

Too many ideals can be dangerous
as Good King Wenceslas found out:
dull bureaucracy not a sharp knife
was the weapon dreaded by Kafka.

Yet I've laughed with soldier Svejk
while the Vltava shone like crystal
and in that Prague Spring of 1968
Palach and Dubcek won our hearts.

A quarter century later and I find
high mass sung now in sv Mikulas.
Holy, holy, lord of the free market
selling korunas to holiday-makers.

Up on the hill a poet president sits
'Havel na Hrad' behind blank walls:
Is it a new world in central Europe
or older music of the usual sphere?

xi

Bealtaine

(1 May)

The International Hotal, [1880s].

(Lawrence collection, Cabinet no. 870)

Monster hotel

Erected,
'on the most extensive plan
of American hotel accommodation'
it finally fell
and left questions
hanging in the sea air.

They stood
and sat there
staring at the camera
feeling no need to smile
for photographs
funeral or circus?
those men
of little expectation
as though pulled up
removing the remains
of a time before railways
before imperial splendour
stuffed into their mourning
stuffed into a modern world
those boys
on donkeys
placid
those beasts
ready to bolt if needs be
man and beast thirsty for drink.

They came
my parents
when
newly-wed
to bed
and board
and spent
during war
a night
at Bray
in 1942
what
secrets
hotel walls
shroud!
What
dreams
and tears
and seed of
conception?

They gaped
how did
that fire
really
start,
and end
engulfing
the hotel?
Newsreels
show
a digger
battering
the shell
with glee,
estimates
covering a
destruction
of Victorian
elegance
in shame.

A stage:
The stagecoach and its load
The young couple and their future
The pan and
grease blazing up:
what mystery in that?

Seeds awake from slumber

Oisín was born
on a clear and breezy day
first child of mine
among the common clutter
of maternity
in a too busy hospital
which smelt of milk and science.

Holding her hand
I watched him come
out of his mother's womb
and felt
the brightened air
striking his curious face
until he was put to breast.

And walking
down a corridor
and out of doors
I raised my head
my body stretching
like a sunflower
towards the source of light.

Opening
in receipt of blessings
which stirred
my flesh and bones
my heart awoke
and I looked people in the face
and glimpsed their child within.

In telescopic leap
I saw each one
simultaneous
through stages of development
as babies still
and in their now
as yet until old age.

So short! So short!
So short the span of years
growing without.

Bray boy in Boston

You said there was no poverty
you saw none on TV
viewing Bay Watch and all its beauties
high schools
where the good guys always get the girls
and where no problem
remains unsolved
for long beyond commercial breaks
where drunks are cheerful
and the sun shines
on white people
and their coloured friends
those kids been there done that:
and everyone has cars
and bright and shiny homes
it's really cool.

Have we a dollar bill with us?
don't mind the guns
they're not intended for the likes of us
just a dollar
to free a baggage trolley which isn't free
you've got to pay here
such is enterprise
we'll reach the highway before long
this traffic jam cannot last
the Sumner tunnel
comes to an end
you are not frightened yet
by all the fuming cars and faces:
beyond some overpass
and by blank shiney towers
America lies.

Pity the man who dies in the storm

Out from behind
the cover of Mars
approaching now
visible.

Origin unknown
the vessel locks on
heading for here
invincible.

Across the galaxies
they know
how we have tended
Earth.

They may not come
to colonise
or to convert
us.

Friend or foe
no defence
as bows and arrows
missiles.

In one swoop
it may end
no nuclear or ozone
suicide.

If we should drown
no ark adrift
who might return
later?

Millions of years
rock hardened
were we the first
here?

One million more
will some Adam
embrace Eve
again?

Tree cheers

Standing aside a calvary,
this sycamore my bodhi be.
with mapled leaves and silver boughs
brain-stemmed and knarled like me.

Furtive suburban   meditation.   car parked
and moment   snatched   from haste.
Up beaten path   and into   clover. Under
  a big tree in the   bushes. Afraid   I might be taken
    for a mugger or a lurker, or be taken by one.
    Not quite the calm and cool collected. Still.
     Better than TV. And seeping in slowly
     stills the brain. The sea, the sky, the grass,
      the life of blowing bushes and the flies
      I did not see before I stopped.
      But flies are busy in this place.
      Still.   Air brush me in. Into a
      space that opens in the boughs
     of sycamore. Five dimensional tree.
    Be comfort for my shoulder while my
feet grow damp and cold among the blades of tufted grass.

I'm not going to help you

- confessions of a guilty bystander

Stopping mid-concourse
staring at noticeboards
reading the times of trains.

Searching for Nijmegen
hearing a plaintive voice
asking me if I'm British.

Feeling my hackles rise
answering too curtly no
seeing a worn Englishman.

Rebuffing his sad story
mouthing I will not help
interrupting his stream.

Observing his shoulders
watching him shuffle off
making a prompt retreat.

Turning in Amsterdam
regretting it got too much
feeling an Irish guilt.

Retracing my steps
willing to listen now
finding him gone away.

Wondering who he was
hating what I had done
asking forgiveness.

What
use is
history on
a rising hill?

So,
who
first
asked
a question
about the past?
When did it flicker
across what consciousness?
Who raised their chin and wondered
how they had come to climb upon some hill?
Why are we here, where are we and where from?
And who will one day ask the last question about what's been,
enquiring what it was all about before it is finally all over and out?

We who were absent lie like eye-witnesses that we know the past
we grasp at answers as the shipwrecked sailor clings to driftwood
creating stories to justify ourselves and to explain the way we are.

Whether or not we call this place by ancient fort or rising ground
or neck or trout or Gaelic clan the story of Bray points to a reality
in time and space where we bend towards happiness out of chaos.

What's she smiling at?

Just around the corner from the world's most famous museum,
on the Rue du Louvre large but ageing neon letters proclaim
the office of 'Detective Du Lac'

O Detective Du Lac,
bureau on Rue du Louvre,
are you inclined to know
why Mona Lisa smirks so?
Could it be, would it be
a clear case of
cherchez l'homme -
just what is she thinking
as she stares out?
Perhaps there's a scandal
involving some madame,
not so much cherchez l'homme
as cherchez la femme.
Or maybe sweet Mona
thinks that God's gonna
bless her especially
and shag all the rest.
Maybe she's simply sweet,
or had something nice to eat.
Did someone die she hated?
Perhaps she's just constipated.
O Detective Du Lac,
do look now, don't be slack,
see if our enigma
just needs some enema.
What kind of dick are you
if you don't give a screw
that the Giaconda's key
cannot be turned?
Thousands of tourists come,
and stand in rain and sun,
waiting to see her smile,
just once for them.
If I'd been Jack Lang,
I'd not have let her hang,
where she drives men astray
passing the time of day,
smiling like that.

xii

Midsummer

Bray Esplanade, looking south, [c. 1890].

(Lawrence collection, Royal no. 399)

Midsummer

Rose of Erin,
flower of June warmth
and longest light,
clear evening stretched to midnight
and sun rising slowly on calm seas.

Blaze bright my love
that you were born
one Summer's day in 1953:
the seed then planted
has been scattered.

It was the year
John Kennedy married Jacqueline
and Marilyn Monroe got pinned to walls
when Gael Linn and An Tostal
protected Irish culture.

Yet Busarus was a sign
of how change intervenes,
opening as your mother delivered you
it is now a rendezvous
for her last widowed outings.

Waiting for Godot on a Paris stage
as you entered
the modern world
where Castro had been jailed
another wheel set to revolve.

This year the summer's sun
shines on uncertainty
and tigers to be tamed
far from the Everest Hillary took
the year Catherine was born.

Here on this headland
where every St John's Eve
they used to set fires blazing
I celebrate my fortune
at full-tide.

Possession

Seized by desire
for her strong, soft, warm,
and sweat-ripening body
in the tulip
of a deep dazzling cotton dress
I'd gotten her for taking off,
wanting a complete conjunction,
I blew it.

I needed her, not dinner,
no starter, main course or dessert,
but dinner was a decency
by the sluggish waters of that city,
and I might be indulged
if she could be impressed.

So
overloaded
by the smell
and look of Lisbon
and its wines,
ready to sink into a bed
of still starched
white linen,
to have her come
again
to meet her heat
and feel her hair
across my face and chest,
cool curves upon my thighs,
I yet found strength to call a taxi
and made for Belem.

There
between the navigators
and their proud tower
where plants were hung
a full moon rose
and in an open window
by the Tagus
it bathed her skin in milk
while candles danced
and her lips curled moist
around the vinegar and oils of Portugal.

Each bite bitten
and enjoyed
the bitter coffee
drunk
we walked
again we walked
as earlier we'd walked
I did not want to walk
no decency was needed now
I felt
near Estoril,
where once my parent's parents
came.

I wanted fusion
I could not stand to see this history
what did I care for power,
for Royal Palace,
let's walk on, I said,
around the Imperial Square
and Fountain of Light
pink and beautiful in the gathering night
and warm air to the train steps.

My eagerness was too eager
and she went to the quay
where fishermen hooked their bait.
and sat in the dress
that I had given her.
I should have let her be
but I complained
and in that chiming of a bell
the hour grew late.

Under the outstretched arms of Christ,
a petulant, grasping, wheedling,
of disturbance and dread
and self-destruction
met a wall and
she, if ever,
no longer
then felt
like me.

Rearing children

Will we wax poetic about child-rearing,
the weekend spent flying solo as father
when mother disappears upon a course
and I am left to cook and mend and do?

I swear I shall appreciate it better how
the usual work of women's really hard
taking in their stride the simple things,
meals and dishes, clothes and shopping.

Minding three children is an endurance
but they have borne it in good humour.
Yet the strain shows when she's absent
and I don't like what it turns up in me.

In them there is a want that I don't fill
gush as I might and try my too hardest
and in myself rises a ready impatience
too quick to spark in an expectant face.

Women with jobs who try to raise kids,
working men who cherish the children,
coming to bed at the tired end of a day,
partners in release, combatants in love.

In the new order of couples scrambling
to satisfy some career or material need
working outside the home seems moral
and may not be deemed a sort of greed.

In the perfect society politically correct
women might share men's every strain
hustling to die younger on average too,
while men reared children just as well.

Perhaps we men should share our jobs
forgo money or status for better things
keeping the children out of institutions
devoted to high standards of child-care.

Yet being unsure of what is best for all
we try to make the most of everything
chasing full lives or finding life too full
our children baffled by our busy round.

116

What is possible

That old frisson
no too slight sensation
but thrill when
someone you'd known
makes contact.

It fills you out
to recall and fantasise
that he or she
was, was not or might
yet cannot be.

That fondness
a touch remembered
and the curve
of bodies in embrace
pressed round.

Now a reserve
but yet warmth here
the eye dance
and the smell of him
or her smiling.

Tangents then
we had crossed going
separate ways
and parting moved on
to come again.

Oh to have all
the then and present
both and each.
those myriad choices
we don't have!

Decision made
gladdening deepening
even a wonder
no end to the possible
except what is.

le trou noir

Black private holes

Wormholes

pulsing

swirling like Zairean girls

dancing

with gravity

pulling time

and curving sp^{a}ce

multiple singularities

beyond the blue

v o i d

It is

so easy to explain

there is you cannot see

(no mystery?)

just one big

bang

(where?)

and then adrift

100,000,000,000

stars

with planets

(none like ours?)

spinning away

dilating in the dark

a cosmic orgasm

Physicists & astronomers

expanding

letting their tongues loose

probing

sniffing on hind legs

the secret recesses of the universe

And the red light

for Niall Quinn.

When I saw sunrise over the Mississippi Delta
I assumed I must have slept:
naked and smiling and standing on a veranda,
she recognised my dreaming.

The sailor walked into a magic Brazilian hotel
embracing his great pleasure:
crouched alone against a wall he hit the bottle
his towel draped on his neck.

In New Orleans the merest glimpse of promise
where I fattened my dreams:
mouths wide and kind and yearning for a kiss
living on credit and favours.

A girl in every port and a room for every girl
but find a table in the room:
on the table pen and paper to catch stolen air
light as a feather but harsh.

The world is an oyster doused in expectations
and some will find a pearl:
but inequity in personal and foreign relations
with iniquity breaks hearts.

The sailor longed to plug the gaping bitterness:
it was his fate and destiny
to search and find what he could not suppress,
his answers mocked at ease.

Deluxed among the gun-shops and great malls
I sat and overeating dinner,
considered the American dream a load of balls
a mad ad trick of television.

The sailor hugged a woman and he read books.
warming to Brendan Behan:
driven to self-destruction by drink and crooks
apt fellow for a borstal boy.

119

The last train to San Fernando is gone long ago
and many people missed it:
yet they stand still trying to see its lights glow
and craving for consolation.

Among the people sits the sailor seeing too far
into a red light of his mind:
endlessly peeling the sad onion of phenomena
in the blue light of feelings.

Is there one good man or woman in Gomorrah
relating a story that is true?
Who may be spared that awful fire tomorrow
if lies and greed are bared?

Our Oedipus at sea recoiled from his own kind,
willing all fatherlands dead:
scarcely would he have suffered more if blind
embracing his mother earth.

When I saw sunrise over the Mississippi River
I assumed that I had dreamt:
the fly on the wall and that sound of laughter
and the bluebottle in the jar.

xiii

Atlantis

Labourer's cottage, [c. 1890].

(Lawrence collection, Royal no. 1785)

Exact location unknown

Welcome to the world!

I love the vigour of that city,
its hey man - what the fuck!
and confidence in tomorrow,
wild crazy jumble of its races
and all the rough and tumble
of its colours, noise and faces.

once from the cockpit of a jet
approaching Kennedy airport,
my fists sweaty and clenched,
I ran to the New York skyline
leaping, electric on a runway.

and seeing a yellow cab float
on one of its narrow avenues,
who could not weep with joy.
being in an old familar place?

the movies gave us America:
their big stories and dreams
rhyming with our own lives.

going home to New York City,
seeing its cruelty and its pity.

what is old world, what new?

Newgrange to New Mexico

Try then to bury our lost innocence?
Out under the desert of New Mexico,
in the eyes of the Native Americans,
the genocide piled high on genocide.

Try then to advise them not to pry?
Who maybe living millenia at peace
must understand what we now say,
for all time, - they've been warned!

Try then to fix signs they can read?
We can't undo the dirty deed done:
the box is open and the clocks run,
generations draw breath and wait.

What did they try to teach us then?
Near the banks of the River Boyne,
who, over four thousand years ago,
erected mounds to honour the sun.

Those circles and spirals and loops?
The big triangles and strange loops:
symbols and signs of consciousness,
speaking in riddles down the years.

Long before Egypt had its pyramids,
builders at Knowth and Newgrange
aligned a burial-chamber on a star,
respectful then of the environment.

If, at the winter solstice every year,
December skies are clear at sunrise,
then rays creep in along its passage
lighting the mound's inner sanctum.

Just a few short thousand years ago,
they too decorated their handiwork
with simple marks or basic designs:
Newgrange stands for natural unity.

So what has New Mexico got to say?
What, in ten thousand years hence?
Will future people, stumbling on it,
enter its passages to seek meaning?

There on the walls they'll see signs,
created by today's genius scientists:
will they pause and decipher these
or, like at Newgrange, just walk on?

As at Newgrange, they'll find death,
but not as old bones turned to dust:
in New Mexico the sands are quick,
where we put nuclear waste on ice.

Try then to say we knew not what?
That people once lived with nature,
courting the sun's energy with life?
That we played God to future ages?

Gondola

In that eight minutes it took us
lives hanging from a thread
out on Sulphur Mountain
onwards and upwards
climbing inexorably
too late to say no
to 2,236 metres
we discovered
something
we knew
already:

That opposites attract.
She hated looking down
and I disliked looking up
so we made a perfect couple
facing across that glass gondola
pulling away from Banff and Bow
thrilling as 9,000,000 more before
finding in nature a cement restaurant
where I had pancakes and she ate fruit.

Coyote

Hearing a coyote cry
in the woods
on Tunnel Mountain

The soft grazing elk
sniffed air
startled and bolted

In the falling night
they ran
finding kith or kin

The Rockies echoed
a lone howl
along the snow line

The cold facts

Oh to begin again and start all over like it never was
and how it's cool up here once more driving to climb
and ride among these wild hard unremitting peaks
and snows where bears and wolves still roam the
wilderness you're warned and on and up through
goat-trekked desert then until a nose bleeds and we
reach a post high outside Jasper and there find
transport to the glacier oh so fresh so fresh but
shattered glass to cut and cold to feel and sense and
walk upon the sounds in all surrounding blue sky
rimmed by rocks and smiles and sun and numbing air
and running water calmness of this ice out of it rivers
pouring to the oceans in the north and east and west
the streams of torquoise flowing down to feed
Atlantic, Arctic and Pacific yet let me be let me just
stand where melting away beneath my feet and up
ahead drops down Columbian Icefield while
underneath the Athabasca Glacier slides a thousand
deep and all at once away where I am standing with
my loves and hugging on this frozen valley floor at
seven thousand feet remembering an age before it all
began and how it may one day all end.

Seattle rattle

On 'five' down to Seattle we knew we'd made it,
almost the West Coast, driving so hard and fast.
Yes! Hey man! This is it. Nirvana by the Pacific.
From Bing and Kurt, from Bertolucci and coffee,
Boeing jets, and fishing, we formed that vision.
But we'd been warned, back in Vancouver, B.C.,
that when in the U.S.A. it can be rough on folks.
It took us a while to get beyond the Peace Gate:
'May this never be closed': but border is border
and they wanted to stamp paper and to see I.D.
We watched as one woman had her auto seized,
arguing 'it is mine' but 'it's ours now' they said:
so laconic, whattagas, sounding just like on T.V.
Waiting we began to count the faces of the kids
'missing and missing', then 'missing and found',
then 'missing and murdered', or 'assassinated'.
'Where are you going?' queried the welcomers:
one of them, smiling and too fat, began to chat,
aghast to hear a mention of Pike Place Market.
'You don't want that', he warned us rightaway,
'it's not safe for children', and 'have a nice day'.

On 'five' down to Seattle we knew we'd made it.
almost the West Coast, driving so hard and fast.
Yes! Hey man! This is it. Nirvana by the Pacific.
Back there in Canada where roads are smooth,
that fella at the filling station said it had been,
'years since I went down there. Bump! Bump!'.
His arms flailed and I must've looked puzzled,
so he explained, 'roads made out of concrete!'.
Turned out he was right. Rattling into the U.S.,
richest economy but lousy roads and welfare.
The stampede gets furious as we travel south,
on Interstate 'five' in the State of Washington.
The drivers may be going nowhere in a hurry,
but I'd sure prefer they'd do it not so near me.
In automobiles and trucks making a mad dash,
will they sweep on through Seattle, by Oregon,
then keep on truckin' to California and Mexico,
running from that dark man on First Avenue?
Once in this stream it's hard to swim to shore:
seeking out our exit I lose my nerve and flee,
getting off the highway the first chance I see.

On 'five' down to Seattle we knew we'd made it,
this North-West Coast, driving so hard and fast.
Yes! Hey man! This is it. Nirvana by the Pacific,
cascade of coke swirling under Mount Olympus.
Over that over-pass where they'd shot Buddha,
down dropping by Madison towards Elliott Bay:
harassed drivers, some shouting, some honking,
high on imported coffee, just loving that city so.
Along the waterfront, by cheap derelict hotels,
to Pioneer Square, as friendly waitress stiffs us.
Pretty neat and blushing, she calls it 'a mistake'
but I think, 'never give a sucker an even break'.
On pizza and ice-creams we survived Pike Place
to pile back into our Hertzmobile and get on out
and catch what's latest on the O.J. Simpson case.
You search for America in its concrete and glass,
in myriad shades and features of its passers-by:
the U.S. flags fluttering in defiance of definition.
Seattle is America's finest and most fashionable,
city of a country powerful and rich and culpable.
beacon in sleepless night. Nirvana by the Pacific.

The waves of the ocean

I know a beach beyond the Rockies:
And the waves of the ocean sparkle.

Go out by Victoria on an island road
And the waves of the ocean sparkle.

Soft doe looked sweet and ran away
And the waves of the ocean sparkle.

Flowers of a new world all in bloom
And the waves of the ocean sparkle.

Pull over where the beach huts run
And the waves of the ocean sparkle.

The Olympic Mountains rise beyond
And the waves of the ocean sparkle.

There sand is warm under bare feet
And the waves of the ocean sparkle.

White wood adrift on pinkish stones
And the waves of the ocean sparkle.

Paddle and play by the wide Pacific
And the waves of the ocean sparkle.

Beyond the horizon went yesterday
And the waves of the ocean sparkle.

And the waves of the ocean sparkle.

And the waves of the ocean sparkle.

And the waves of the ocean sparkle.

xiv

Lughnasa

(1 August)

Little Bray, [*c.* 1890].

(Lawrence collection, Royal no. 1677).

From the Maltings, left,
across the River Dargle
to the old castle in Little Bray

Grist to whose mill?

Sam Naylor's salmon hatched in the waters of an old
millrace that ran by the ancient Norman mill of Bray
and nudged its wheel while horses grazed on millfield
grass. And down between the Crab and Periwinkle
rocks at Naylor's Cove the people came to bathe from
wood and canvas booths and trains ran up the head to
let the swimmers off at a half-platform under Fiddler's
Bridge. Along the seafront once stood a Martello
Tower, its comrade still standing near the harbour.
And from the square end to the round the slow and
easy trains ran out of Bray and by Shankhill on past
Foxrock and into Harcourt Street. And a little stone
castle gave its name to Castle Street, nothing too grand
but a marker for the town of Bray. A charming lodge
set off the People's Park of Little Bray, in tribute to
Victorian taste And jolly chair-planes lifted hearts up
to The Eagle's Nest.

A while ago they filled the race against advice and on
the field built tax-efficient houses. At Naylor's Cove
long since they put in cement seabaths and bunkers
before leaving the lot to rot. Now no train stops at the
fully over-grown half-platform. The Martello Tower
went a century ago lest it mar the look of the
Esplanade (a consideration lost on those who recently
approved the aquarium and shops and added a new
car-park). And a servant of the Republic closed the
slow and easy line, tearing up tracks so no West Brit
elite or native green might ever ride that way again.
The little castle was knocked for a supermarket car-
park. The lodge was left to vandalism until one night it
burned and the way was cleared for a new bridge
through the People's Park (but this was stopped by
public outcry). And jolly chair-planes rusted so their
pulleys pull no more.

Brunel's folly

When I was all of seven,
at kindergarten,
Miss Dolan put me in charge
and left the room.

Pacing back and forth,
important I
banged my exalted crown
on the fireplace.

'Ah, pride takes a fall!',
she croaked,
returning to her domain
of infant school.

Such a harsh lesson
Brunel learnt
driving his railway line
past Bray Head.

That great engineer
overstretched,
his impermanent way
set for a tumble.

Elbowed to seaside,
by Lord Meath,
his fame foundered
on Cambrian rock.

Gerald

Did I meet Gerald of Braybroke
standing by Brabazon Corner?
Who was this Gerald who came
walking past as I stared down?
I told a tale of wooden viaduct
and engine jumping the tracks
and two dying in August 1867.
It is a gloomy and a dank place,
so spectres rise readily to mind
of dead and of severely injured
lying in pain remote from help
on a summer morning in 1867.
He spoke of time and ignorance
and we discussed the universe
and life and death and honesty.
Then standing on that cold path
below the ancient weeping cliff
he talked to me of astral plains
and of dreams of reincarnation,
holding his shades in the gloom.

Gerald told of being here before
while I shivered at the thought
that there could have returned
a passenger or the train driver,
guilty ganger or his supervisor.
Reading *Fireside Tales of Death*,
he had recognised himself in it
and in a dream was confirmed
as reborn Gerald of Braybroke:
'and I was broke then,' he said,
'when I used to reside in Bray!'
But this had rung a bell for me,
summoning up another Gerald
bound for war never to return,
leaving my grand-aunt bereft.
Yet I did not interrupt his flow
as he told of a dream in which
in a former life he filed bullets
and boarded a train to combat,
sure there would be no return.

Accident at Ram's Scalp bridge, Bray Head
The Illustrated London News, 24 August 1867

Dún Brea

there are soft mysteries
in the story of each free hill
although the sídhe are dismissed
and under the rising ground between
this river and this headland known as Bray
is buried Brea, protector of Partholon, so it's said.
Brea, son of Both of perpetual valour, maker of hides
and the constructor of iron vessels of occidental darkness.
Brea, son of Senboth of the spears, got a dún, a river and high sea.
he was not wanton-foolish being first to occupy this strong height.
it was here assuredly died Brea and all his children alongside him.
his great grave with an army assembled around was seen in Cuala.

There was a day

The transmigration of Tuan mac Cairill

There was a day
When it came to pass
As pass it always must
What is old yields to new
As on that morning long ago
When I fought the elders at Brea.

There was a day after the Flood
When Partholon, son of Sera, took Ireland.

True were my words in council
Sweet my song across a dark road
Among the women with beauty there.
Fair my face and swift my step in battle
At Dún Brea when my warriors hurled spears.
Five thousand were of the race of Partholon then
But between two Sundays all mortals died save one.

There was a day when I was old
Nemed, son of Agnoman, my father's brother, came.

With Nemed were four couples
All survivors of a fleet of barques.
Nine of a band lost on the Caspian Sea.
Watching and avoiding I grew wretched,
Grey, hairy, clawed, naked, withered, forlorn.
I saw myself passing into the shape a young stag
Waking from sleep glad to lead the herds of Ireland.

There was a day when I was old
All the issue of that race of Nemed died.

Away from ghostly settlements
Along cliffs or through wilderness
I fled from wolves and came to a cave
And I saw that I was passing once more,
No herd of stags about me as I became a boar,
A mighty lord among boars with great triumphs
Having been put in wonderful grief in many shapes.

There was a day when I was old
Fir Domnann and Fir Bolg of Semion came.

A great sadness came upon me
Unable to effect what I did before
Going the rounds with no strength left
Alone in dark caves and on hidden cliffs.
I remembered how it was I altered my shape
And going to that abode where always I changed
I went into the shape of a big hawk eager and lusty.

There was a day when I was old
The wonderful Tuatha Dé Danaan came.

And my mind was again happy
Flying over everything in Ireland
A hawk to-day but a boar yesterday,
Awesome inconstancy of God my maker!
Dearer each day is the Friend who shaped me
He is my help even as demons rule Nemed's issue
And I know that I shall yet pass into another shape.

There was a day when I was old
The sons of Mil took Ireland from the Tuatha Dé Danann.

I remained a hawk at that time
In the hollow of a tree by a river
Till sleep there and then fell upon me
And I passed into the shape of a salmon.
Once more I felt happy, vigorous and well-fed.
My swimming was good and I escaped all danger,
Although I still bear all the scars of hunters' spears.

There was a day when I was old
God deemed it time that I return as a human being.

Then beasts were pursuing me,
I was known by all the fishermen,
And so I was caught for Cairell's wife.
That queen had a desire to eat some fish
So they put me on a gridiron and roasted me.
She ate me by herself so that I was in her womb
And I remember what was said to her or done then.

There was a day when I was born
Being named then Tuan, son of Cairell.

I grew up a 'file' being baptised
When Patrick came with his creed.
Then was learning in Gaelic and Latin,
Although the fierce Uí Neills were rough
And always septs were lying in wait for blood.
So rage drove me to kill a Noreseman at Clontarf
Yet tears led me for a penance to Uí Briúin Cualann.

There was a day when I was old
Strongbow, Richard de Clare, came with his Normans.

To avoid the men from the east
I had not strength in foot or hand.
But I passed into the shape of an owl.
A castle rose within earshot of Dún Brea
And I flew high over its cornmill and millrace
Watching as settlers became more Irish each day.
Wonderfully did the turning of a wheel dispose me.

There was a day when I was old
Tudor, Stuart and Hanoverian forces came.

I saw myself change into a deer
Fleeing the hunter from hill to hill
Captured for sport in Brabazon's park.
Life was devoted to evading destruction.
Great my grief while Ireland remained empty
Ravaged by foreign armies, brutality and famine.
Persecution, division and acrimony stalked the land.

There was a day when I was old
When warriors declared Ireland free.

I watched them from the wood
Being miserable, weak and broken.
But then, asleep, I saw myself passing
Into the shape of a young and wild hare
And I ran as they fought amongst themselves
Not only Gaelic but also descended of other races
Learning new ways as comes to any man or woman.

There was a day
When it came to pass
As pass it always must
What is old yields to new
As on that morning long ago
When I fought the elders at Brea.

I, Tuan, son of Cairell, son of Muredach
I who have conversed with Colum Cille
And who know the histories of Ireland.

Idol chatter

If this book is a statue it may not pass the door
of that basilica in Paris of Saint Julien-the-Poor.

A statue seems to mimic sacred flesh and blood
and must not be adored when only God is good.

Works of art may lie, in paint or words or earth,
being shaped by a mortal, of little lasting worth.

But the orthodox use icons, symbols of the best,
a guide for the hopeful to that which is blessed.

My book is an impression, sketched upon a wall,
of slender faith in graces, to save us from a fall.

Bray Head Hotel, [c. 1886].

(Lawrence collection, Royal no. 459)

Raheenaclig church is visible on the hill.

Notes

Bray Head and sea front, [c. 1886].

(Lawrence collection, Royal no.1688).

Bray

Bray Head in County Wicklow is a high, large, cape, rising up from the banks of the River Dargle and stretching out a considerable way into the sea. Bray has a population of 27,000 people, most of whom live between the river and the headland and many of whom commute to work in Dublin City. Bray Head is at the southern extremity of Dublin Bay, corresponding to Howth Head on the northern side. Trains of 'The DART' (Dublin Area Rapid Transit) shuttle back and forth between Bray and Howth. The town enjoys bookshops, theatre groups, art galleries and a heritage centre with exhibition area. It has also a public library, newspaper, film society, radio station and cinema with four screens.

Possible origins of the name of Bray

i) From the Irish 'brí', meaning a hill or rising ground, or even from 'braighe', meaning neck.

The earliest incontrovertible reference to the Bray area, in the thirteenth century, spells it Bree. Between then and the sixteenth century it was spelt Bree or Bre. The first known use of 'Bray' does not occur until 1530. It may have become spelt in this fashion because the Normans were familiar with a number of other 'Brays' in northern France and England. That this name might, however, be an anglicised version of a Gaelic word was proposed in 1705 by James Ware. Ware described the headland of Bray and suggested that 'perhaps it was so named from some fancied resemblance it bears to a neck, which is "braighe" in Irish, or from "brí", a hill'. Certainly the land rises steadily from the river to the headland and this persuaded Canon Scott in 1913 to concur with Ware on 'brí'. Hogan also seems to support this derivation. However, their explanation was dismissed summarily by Liam Price in 1943, ostensibly on linguistic grounds.

ii) From the ancient Irish name Dún Brea or Dún Bré, - Brea being a hero in the Celtic mythological history of Ireland.

The identification of Bray with the ancient 'Dún Brea' has been firmly suggested by, amongst others, Osborn Bergin of U. C. D. in 1927 and Liam Price in 1943. Price was a president of the Royal Society of Antiquaries in Ireland and an authority on Wicklow place-names.
The text of the mythological version of the origins of the name Dún Brea, recorded almost one thousand years ago in the 'Dindshenchas', is reworked above in the poem 'Dún Brea'. The original text indicates that Dún Brea was visible from Howth, was south of the Liffey and encompassed a dún, a burial mound, a river or river-harbour and a stretch of 'noble' or high sea. One problem faced by Price in equating Bray with Dún Brea was the absence of any known fortified mound or 'dún' in the Bray area.
Price suggested imaginatively that a place known formerly as 'Fairy Hill', where Galtrim Park now stands on the south-east side of Bray bridge, was the original Dún Brea. The existence of a very old Christian site nearby, where St Paul's church stands, lends some weight to his theory.
However, Price himself noticed in a different context a reference by Curry in 1838 to a site in Ballynamuddagh townland, at Windgate[s] on the back of Bray Head, which was known as 'The Giant's Grave', - although 'no vestige of a grave remains' wrote Curry for the ordnance survey. If there was an important grave there, might there not also have been a dún in the vicinity, perhaps visible from the sea and giving its name to the area below it? In fact, it has been suggested that there was a promontory fort on the cliffs at Cable Rock. Even a fort high on the back of the head would overlook part of Dublin Bay. There are other indications that the headland may indeed have been not only the site of a grave but of Dún Brea itself.
Firstly, the account in the 'Dindshenchas' refers to Dún Brea in the context of 'five strong heights' or hills. The first of these is the hill of Etar or Howth and the second is Dún Brea. Is it likely that this would be meant to refer to a lowly dún near the river, rather than to some elevated place? Anyone sailing into Dublin Bay in fine weather is struck immediately by the two corresponding headlands of Howth and Bray.
Secondly, in the 'Book of Howth', Windgate gets mentioned in the context of a list of strongholds and Price believes that this particular reference has 'some connection' to that reference in the standard account of the Battle of Ventry to an 'Inibhir Breagh rea raidhtear Bearna Gaoithe'.

In this context too it is worth noting that James Ware has left us an enigmatic and hitherto unnoticed reference to a monument at Windgate which must almost certainly be the 'Giant's Grave'. In his *Antiquities*, which appeared in London in an English version in 1705, the old Irish custom of burying notable individuals 'under a heap of stones' is discussed:

> If according to this custom that heap of stones at Windgate in the county of Wicklow were not laid there in memory of the slain, it may seem to be a mercurial monument, laid there by travellers according to the custom of antiquity, in honour of Mercury [Lugh], the protector of travellers, or one of those heaps of stones which were heretofore laid to design the mears and bounds of lands and were called scorpions.

Harris, editing an edition of Ware in 1745, described this heap of stones as 'vast'. There is a strange story about a 'grave' at 'bearna na gaoithe' (Windgate) in the 'Account of Saint Maignenn of Kilmainham', written in the fifteenth century. Maignenn had flourished about AD 600. The only 'bearna na gaoithe' given by Hogan is that near Bray. Maignenn is said to have passed bearne na gaoithe without noticing 'a cross and a fresh grave' there. When told about these he immediately returned:

> for a long space he was in contemplation of the cross and of the grave; nor spoke to any, but to the cross bent the knee three times. His people questioned him, what made him to be silent; he never answered them; a three hours' spell he continued so, then in a voice mild and gentle said: 'I charge thee tell me who is laid in that grave; and what the reason that I never saw the cross, and I after passing close beside it'. The miserable being answering him said: 'I will tell thee that, holy bishop, even though from thy interpellation I gain no relief. I am a heathen, and never was it feasible to do evil but I did it; the weak I harried, I sought to curry favour with the strong; on the feeble churches I exercised persecution, and incurred excommunication by bell and candle with malediction of the righteous; I had death without penitence, and all philosophers of the world could not recite the one half of my torment unless that Almighty God should tell it. Wherefore it is, holy bishop, that the guardian angel thou hadst with thee suffered thee not to see me; and by God I adjure thee now, holy bishop, pray for me and bestow on me thy mercy!' Thereupon, Maignenn looked up to God, but his guardian angel said to him: 'rouse not God's wrath, neither any more idly waste thy time'. Maignenn made a genuflection, and by the same path returned back to the place where Moling was.

Taking these accounts with Curry's mention of a 'Giant's Grave' and the references in the 'Dindshenchas' and 'Book of Howth' to 'Brea', it seems reasonable to assume that on Bray Head may have stood 'Dún Brea'. It may be noted that just south of Bray Head lay the old Gaelic centre of Rathdown.

iii). From the O'Brien sept name, 'Uí Briúin Cualann'.

Between AD 500 and AD 1000 this Gaelic sept came to occupy those parts of what is now north Wicklow and south Dublin which were earlier known as Cuala or Cualainn. There is no authority for supposing that the form 'Bree' derived from this sept name. However, the association of the locality with this Gaelic family took the fancy of Bray local authority in the early years of the Irish Free State and amid some controversy in 1927 they adopted 'Brí Chualann' as the Irish form of the town's name.

147

The name of Bray

iv). From a root of Bri-ghid, Bri-gantes, Br-an, Bre-ga, Bri-ton?

Is it possible that the name might derive from those figures of the Celtic pantheon later subsumed into St Brighid and St Brendan? Brighid was known as Brigantia to the Brigantes tribe, which was settled in south Leinster. Raheenaclig church is said to have been known as St Brendan's. The territory of Brega is associated with the modern Co. Meath but its southern boundary appears once to have reached the River Liffey.

About a century before Christ, the Greek Ptolemy wrote a geography of Ireland in which he listed among the tribes of Ireland the 'Cauci', then living around what is now the North Wicklow area. O'Rahilly suggests that it is 'most likely' that Ptolemy was in fact referring to the Cualainn, who were part of the Builg, commonly called Fir Bolg, also known as Erainn, who constituted the second of four waves of Celtic migration into Ireland. The Builg appear to be of the same stock as were the Britons.

Éber, son of Míl, was one of the mythical ancestors of the southern Goidels, part of the fourth Celtic migration. Although, as we have seen, the Cualainn were seemingly part of an earlier Celtic invasion, it was suggested by some ancient genealogists that the Cualainn were also descended from Éber. Might Dún Brea, therefore, be a version of Éber Donn?

v). From the profusion of trout in the river?

Long before the river through Bray became known as the Dargle it was known as Bray River or Bray Water, right up to one of its sources at Lough Bray in Glencree. It was long considered a very good river for trout. The Gaelic for trout is 'breac', of which the g. s. m. (as in 'river of trout') is 'bric'. A small trout is 'bricín'. This is admittedly an unlikely explanation.

vi). From the fact that earliest inhabitants lived close to nature and decided that the name Bray, in whatever form, felt right!

Sources: James Ware, *The antiquities and history of Ireland* (London, 1705), p.153; James Ware, 'Antiquities' in *Works concerning Ireland, revised and improved*, ed. Walter Harris (2 vols., Dublin, 1739 and 1745), ii, 140-41, 202; 'Account of Saint Maignenn of Kilmainham' (British Library, Egerton MS 91, ff 49-51), translated at Standish O'Grady (ed.), *Silva Gadelica: a collection of tales in Irish edited from manuscripts and translated* (2 vols, London, 1892), ii, 42-43; Colum Kenny, *Kilmainham: the history of a settlement older than Dublin* (Dublin, 1995), ch. 1, 'An account of Saint Maignenn'; Letter from Eugene Curry, 27 Dec. 1838, in 'Ordnance survey letters, 1839' (National Library of Ireland typescript, Ir 9141o24, pp. 28-9, 36); Edmund Hogan, *Onomasticon Goedelicum: an index to Gaelic names of places and tribes* (Dublin and London, 1910), p.122; Canon George Digby Scott, *The stones of Bray* (Dublin, 1913, reprinted Bray 1984), pp. 96-98, 218-21, 231-32; Liam Price, 'The name of Bray' in *Eigse*, iv (1943), 147-51; Liam Price, 'The grant to Walter de Ridelesford of Brien and the land of the sons of Turchill' in *R.S.A.I.Jn.*, lxxxiv (1954), 72-73; Liam Price, *Place-names of Wicklow, v* (Dublin, 1957, reprinted 1983), pp. 326-27; Thomas F. O'Rahilly, *Early Irish History and Mythology* (Dublin, 1976), pp. 14-17. 24-29, 197-99; Niall O Dónaill and Tomás De Bhaldraithe (ed.), *Foclóir Gaeilge-Béarla* (Dublin, 1977), pp. 134, 140; 'Letters' in *Irish Times*, 11, 12, 14, 18 and 19 May 1927; The friends of historic Rathdown, *Ancient Rathdown and Saint Crispin's Cell: a uniquely historic landscape* (Greystones, 1993), p. 9, p. 12; Brian White, 'The name "Bray" is known far and wide' in *Bray People*, 3 February 1995; below, p.158 for more on Dún Brea.

Riding high: Sir George Radcliffe was master of the rolls in Ireland and secretary to the lord deputy, Sir Thomas Wentworth (Black Tom). In the 1630s Radcliffe created a deerpark at Downs, east of Kilruddery, near Bray. When Wentworth fell, having incurred the enmity of all factions in Ireland, Radcliffe was arrested and imprisoned in London. His admittance to new chambers at King's Inns, Dublin, was 'to stand ensuing the absence of the said Sir George out of this kingdom', to which he never in fact returned. The judges' chambers at King's Inns were strewn with herbs from its garden (Rolf Loeber, 'Settlers utilisation of the natural resources' in Ken Hannigan and William Nolan (eds), *Wicklow: history and society* (Dublin, 1994), p. 272; Colum Kenny, *King's Inns and the Kingdom of Ireland: the Irish 'inn of court' 1541-1800* (Dublin, 1992), pp.112-14).

Why Bray? The quotation at the top of the poem is from Samuel Beckett's *Murphy*. Also Beckett's is the description of the outlook at Bray as 'Beautiful view all bare and glitter' (Kilcool [sic] ms cited at S.E. Gontarski, *The intent of undoing in Samuel Beckett's dramatic texts* (Bloomington, 1985), p.136). 'Noble sea' is from the Dindshenchas.
     For some possible explanations of the name of Bray see above.

Them and us: Colbert Martin, 'Victorian pillar-boxes' in *Bray Hist. Record*, i (1986), pp. 37-39; Stanislaus Joyce, *My brother's keeper (London, 1958)*, p. 31; Flynn, *Bray*, p. 75, p. 82.

Picnic at Redford Cemetery: The author worked as a waiter in Portsmouth, N.H., in 1970 and 1972. Shanganagh cemetery lies near the sea between Bray and Shankill. Buried there is Michael B. Kenny (1919-92), a life member of the 'Pioneer Total Abstinence Association of the Sacred Heart'. Samuel Beckett is said to have enjoyed visiting graveyards and lunching among the headstones. His parents are buried in Redford Cemetery, at the foot of the southern slope of Bray Head and he wrote of picnicking there (Deirdre Blair, *Samuel Beckett* (London, 1978), pp. 300-01; Eoin O'Brien, *The Beckett Country* (Dublin, 1986), pp. 98-104).

Standing on Bray Head: 'Om mani padme hum' is a Tibetan mantra which expresses respect for life and for the ground of our being. 'Dia duit, agus dóchas freisin' means 'God be with you, and hope also'.

Another mountain: Cézanne is known to have painted Mont Sainte Victoire in Provence on scores of occasions. The description of him as 'poetic...' is by his contemporary Baille. For guidance on Cézanne I am especially indebted to Nicholas Wadley, *The Paintings of Cézanne* (London, 1989).

Conceal not the blood: 'Earth conceal not the blood shed on thee' is the epitaph on the memorial at the site of Belsen. concentration camp. For a general introduction to the history of the Bray area see Scott, *Stones of Bray*, pp. 1-25; Alfred P. Smyth, *Celtic Leinster: towards an historical geography of early Irish civilization A.D. 500-1600* (Dublin, 1982), pp. 50-56; Flynn, *Bray*, pp 12-22; Tony Dunne, 'The physical geography of North County Wicklow' and Leo Swan, 'Prehistoric and early Christian Bray' in *The Book of Bray*, pp. 3-6, 21-25; Linzi Simpson, 'Anglo-Norman settlement in Uí Briúin Cualann, 1169-1350' in Hannigan and Nolan, *Wicklow*, pp. 191-235.

The earliest literary reference to Bray ['bree'] occurs in a late thirteenth century poem found among the Carew manuscripts at Lambeth Palace. Translated it reads, 'He gave him [Maurice, son of Fitzgerald] too Wicklow, Between Bray and Arklow; This was the land of Kill Mantain, Between Ath-Cliath [Dublin] and Loch Garman [Wexford]' (G. H. Orpen (ed.), *The song of Dermot and the Earl* (Oxford, 1892), pp. 132-3, 224-5). The legend has it that King James, routed at the battle of the Boyne, stopped a night at Puck Castle. The castle, just north of Bray, is now a dangerous ruin. Smyth writes that 'in Celtic times, the otherwise very diverse tribes of the Fortuatha Laigen ('alien people amongst the Leinstermen') of the Wicklow massif were grouped collectively under that name in recognition of their special political and geographical status among the Wicklow Hills' (Alfred P. Smyth, 'Kings, saints and sagas' in Hannigan and Nolan, *Wicklow*, p.44).

Bray opera house: In the early twentieth century the wealthy Sir Stanley Cochrane built at Woodbrook House, near Little Bray, what was intended to be an indoor cricket ground but what became briefly an opera house. James Joyce, aged about six, took part with his parents in an amateur concert at Bray Boat Club, which was near their home in Martello Terrace. More recent residents of this terrace have included the conductor Roger Doyle, singer Mary Coughlan, film director Neil Jordan and government minister, Liz McManus T. D. Cyril Cusack, then a child lodging at 1 Herbert Terrace (the present home of the author), played in the Assembly Rooms in 'Dick Whittington' (Flynn, *Bray*, p. 97; Ellmann, *Joyce*, pp. 26-7).

Off the walls: After the 'official' opening by artist Brian Maguire of an art exhibition by Doug Ross, at the Heritage Centre, Bray, 2 November 1994, hosted by Bray Urban District Council.

Forehead to wave: 'Forehead to wave' is how the 'Dindshenchas' anciently described Howth Head (Gwynn (ed.), *Dindshenchas*, pt.III, p.110).

The dread: The chapel of bones in the church of Sao Francisco in Evora, Portugal, is said to include the bones of 5,000 monks. It is entered under an inscription which states that 'the bones here await your bones'.

Nuit Saint George: In February 1922 *Shakespeare & Company,* Paris, published the first edition of Joyce's *Ulysses.* The company was run by the late Sylvia Beach and is now run by George Whitman. Its stamp contains the words 'kilometer [sic] zero, Paris'. The bookshop, over which for a time was the Tumbleweed Hotel, is one of the cultural landmarks of Paris. In 1984 in New York Garland published a critical and synoptic edition of *Ulysses.*

Les Trompettes of Versailles: 'Les Trompettes of Versailles' perform regularly on the left bank at the ancient church of St Julien-le-Pauvre, which is now in the care of the Orthodox Church. On 12 November 1994 their concert featured pieces by Loeillet, Mozart, Bach, Macello, Corelli, Haydn, Vivaldi and by the organist himself, Georges Bessonnet. The ensemble was born after a concert in the Chapel Royal at Versailles in 1983. The trio give over one hundred concerts in Paris each year.

Christmas on Bray Main Street: Cearbhall O Dálaigh, president of Ireland 1974-76, was born in 1911 at 85 Main Street, now the 'Jasmine House' restaurant (*Journal of the Cualann Historical Society* (1990), pp. 5-8). Peter Regan writes books for young people. Staff of record shops may on occasion be heard saying that they have 'no woman's hearts', in response to a request for the collection of popular songs, 'A Woman's Heart'.

Single market: The main square in Munich, the Marienplatz, was reconstructed following severe Allied bombing. One of its features is the 43-bell Glockenspiel, complete with groups of metal figures.

The cattle: This tribute to the English writer refers to some well-known Hardy works, including 'The Oxen' and 'At Castle Boterel'.

Christmas at Christ's church? Amongst the Christian churches of Bray are Christ Church, The Most Holy Redeemer, St Peter's, St Paul's, St Andrew's and St Fergal's. The quakers used to worship in the town's former Turkish Baths. In 1881 the bells were hung at Christ Church. They had been paid for in part by a subscription from William Gladstone, who visited Kilruddery, Bray, in 1877. Prime Minister Gladstone's Church Act of 1869 had earlier disestablished and disendowed the Anglican Church of Ireland. At the time, Father James Healy, a renowned conversationalist, was a local catholic parish priest, - see *Memories of Father Healy of Little Bray* (three editions to 1898). In 1895 The Most Holy Redeemer was decorated in part by Signor Edward Buccini, a Neapolitan artist living in Bray. The panel of the reredos at Christ Church is filled with a mosaic from the Salviatis Glass Works in Venice. In 1940 the local Presbyterian minister was involved with the catholic parish priest in setting up a turf-cutting scheme which gave employment. Rev. David Godfrey is rector of Christ Church, Bray.

L'Irlandaise: Beckett dubbed the north beach between Greystones and Bray Head, overhung by soft, unconsolidated, glacial cliffs, 'this côte de misère'. For Joyce and Beckett around Bray Head see James Joyce, *A portrait of the artist as a young man* (Chancellor Press ed., London, 1993), pp.134-41; Joyce, *My brother's keeper*, pp. 28-29, 39; Deirdre Bair, *Samuel Beckett* (London,1978), pp. 67-73, 92-101, 297-301. Lucia was Joyce's daughter.

Lucia visited Bray in 1935 and stayed at the bungalow of Joyce's sister, Eileen. Lucia telegrammed her father, 'You look like Bray Head!', and he replied, 'I believe you to be in Ireland but you are also in Norway. The Norwegians founded the city of Wicklow which means: Wick, little harbour, and low, light house' (Ellmann, *Joyce*, p. 697). Price, *Place-names*, vii, xx, says that, 'The name Wicklow means "the water-meadow of the Vikings"').

Treachery: The interview conducted by the author with Cardinal Cahal Daly in Belfast was published in the *Sunday Independent* on 1 Jan. 1995.

Ultra litora Iuverna: In 1835, it is said, workmen levelling a bank of sand towards the southern end of Bray seafront discovered the graves of a number of persons buried in Roman style. On or beside the skeletons were coins of the reigns of Trajan (AD 97-117) and Hadrian (AD 117-138). The skeletons rapidly disintegrated upon exposure, a process graphically described in another case by one Dr Rowan (Dr Rowan cited at John Windele, 'On an ancient cemetery at Ballymacus near Kinsale' in *Kilkenny Archaeological Soc. Transactions*, ii (1852-3), p. 233).

151

The finding of a Roman or Romanised burial site was first reported in 1837 by Lewis, who gave 1835 as the year of the find, and again in 1841 by Dr W. H. Drummond. In 1838, in his report for the ordnance survey, Curry described how 'some old people here remember having seen bones (human), some say skeletons of men, women and children, dug up from a great depth at the edge of the beach, a little within Bray Head; at or near one of the lodges or gate houses belonging to Mr Putland of Dublin'. However, he made no mention of Roman coins and the reference to 'old people' suggests that the discovery to which he referred was much earlier than the decade in which he wrote, notwithstanding apparent similarities in the three accounts. Curry suggests that the graves may have marked the site of Dun Brea! (Lewis, *Topographical dictionary* (Dublin, 1837), sub Bray; *R.I.A.Proc.*, ii (1841), p.186; 'Ordnance survey letters', pp 29-30; K. Mary Davies, 'A note on the location of the Roman Burial site at Bray, Co.Wicklow' in *Archaeology Ireland*, iii, no. 3 (Autumn, 1989), pp. 108-09). Both Arthur Doran, *Bray and environs* (c.1905, facsimile Bray, 1985), p.7 and Scott, *Stones of Bray*, pp. 41-45 gave reign to their imagination to explain how these burials came about).

It used to be said commonly, even thirty years ago, that 'the Romans never reached Ireland' but scholars have recently qualified that view. Besides the traffic in missionary activity, there is also evidence of considerable trade with and even some settlement of Romans. Once, for example, foreshadowing the later relationship between Dermot MacMurrough and the Normans, Agricole welcomed 'an Irish prince who had been driven from home by a rebellion, nominally a friend, he might have been used as a pawn in the game'. Juvenal (cited by Warner) observed that 'arma quidem ultra litora Iuvernae promovimus [Roman arms had been advanced beyond the shores of Hibernia]'. Warner also points out that a highly Romanised group of Irish aristocrats returned to Ireland in the early second century (R.B.Warner, 'Some observations on the context and importation of exotic material in Ireland from the first century B.C. to the second century A.D.' in *R.I.A.Proc.*, lxxvi (1976), C, pp. 279-82; Tacitus, *Agricole*, 24 cited at Edward Bourke, 'Stoneyford, Co.Kilkenny: a first century Roman burial from Ireland' in *Archaeology Ireland*, iii, no.2 (Summer, 1989), pp. 56-57).

For the legend that the seas off Bray Head are haunted by a chief of the O'Byrnes see Colbert Martin, 'The phantom bark' in *Bray Hist. Soc.*, i (1986), pp. 44-45). In 1155-6 the pope approved a Norman invasion of Ireland, ostensibly for the purposes of religious reform.

To go to Rome: Founded by Tibetan buddhist refugees, Samye-Ling is a centre for study, work and meditation. It lies north of the Scottish-English border, in Eskdalemuir. The author first discovered Samye-Ling through reading a footnote in the *Asian Journal* of Thomas Merton and has visited it a number of times during the past two decades. An old Irish proverb says of pilgrimage: 'To go to Rome, great the effort, little the gain: you will not find there the king you seek unless you bring him with you'.

Dun Laoghaire/Holyhead: In 1852 the 'Lady Harriet' was lost off Bray Head. On 1 Sept. 1875 the ironclad 'Vanguard' sank in fog off the Kish Lighthouse. On 30 Sept. 1876 the brig 'Leona', en route for Liverpool from Nova Scotia, was wrecked at Bray Head. On 10 Oct. 1918 the mail steamer 'Leinster' was sunk by a torpedo near the Kish. For more on these and other wrecks see *Bray Historical Record: Journal of the Old Bray Society*, vi (1994), dedicated 'to all those who went down to the sea in ships'.

Bonfires: *Irish Times*, 8 Jan. 1868; Scott, *Stones of Bray*, pp. 76-91; Stanislaus Joyce, *My brother's keeper* ((London, 1958), pp. 33-34; Flynn, *Bray*, pp. 78-80, 95; *Book of Bray*, pp. 45-49. Sir William Brabazon was vice-treasurer and receiver in Ireland, under Henry VIII. In the seventeenth century the Brabazons were created earls of Meath and granted extensive lands at Bray. A deerpark was attached to their house at Kilruddery, behind Bray Head, and the family still holds much land in the area.

Bray water: See *Irish Builder*, 1 Dec. 1893, 15 Nov. 1895; Michael Suttle, 'The story of Bray harbour' in *The Book of Bray*, pp. 99-102).

Spring: The road to Greystones was the royal highway and on the Bray Head side between Bray and Windgate are marvellous sweeping fields of wheat, which run down from an old farm that is powered by wind. A ghost is said to haunt the area.

9 February 1861:   On this date the brig 'Endeavour' disintegrated at Bray. In the same storm five ships went down off Wicklow. To save a fifth man, Lacy lashed him to himself and was hauled ashore by rope: 'Some years ago when I spoke on this brave deed I was promised that some form of monument was going to be erected to their memory but this has not happened so far'. So wrote John de Courcy Ireland in his 'Wreck and rescue off the North Wicklow coast' in *Bray Historical Record*, vi (1994).

Glencree: (*Glean criothaigh* / glen of the shaking bog or morass): High in the Wicklow hills up by Lough Bray, source of the River Dargle, the rambling barracks at Glencree was built following the 1798 rebellion. It lay vacant for many years before the Oblate Order acquired it and established St Kevin's Reformatory (1858-1940). About 300 'delinquents' were housed there in basic conditions and forced to farm 'the surrounding waste'. The Oblates meant it as a refuge rather than a place of punishment. Between 1945 and 1950 it was used as a centre for thousands of Polish and German refugees. Nearby, a cemetery was opened for German servicemen who had died in Ireland. Since 1975 the property at Glencree has been partly developed by the Centre for Reconciliation, of which this author is currently a council member. The old catholic chapel is still in use and there have recently been reports of a statue moving in a wood there. When Oscar (originally 'Oscár') Wilde was a boy his family had a summer cottage in Glencree and Lady Wilde brought Oscar and his brother to mass in the reformatory chapel. It is said she had the boys baptised as catholics there, when Oscar was about six years old The local fortune-teller who forecast Wilde's downfall was known internationally as Cheiro. The first Oscar Wilde Summer School was held in Bray in 1994 (*Ir. Builder*, xxiv, p.281 (1 Oct.1882) for Lough Brays; Price, *Place-names*, v, 282; David McHigh, 'Glencree reformatory: historic building study, 1994'; Richard Ellmann, *Oscar Wilde* (London, 1987), pp. 18-19, 360; Colbert Martin, 'Cheiro' in *Bray Historical Record*, no.1 (1986), pp. 27-28. For Wilde and Bray see Flynn, *Bray*, 128-9).

Templecarrig: This name, in Irish *teampull carraig*, means 'church of the rock'. 'Nothing is known about the church', says Price, who thinks that, 'the exact meaning of the word *teampull* is not clear'. The Master of the Templars held property in the Bray area in 1280. I have taken poetic licence to suggest an origin for the name of this townland just south-west of Bray Head (Price, *Place-names*, pp. 324-25; Scott, *Stones*, p.105).

Mutoscope: William Power was a pioneering Irish film director who also worked as a barber on Novara Road, Bray. A fine Gaumont movie camera, which is thought to have belonged to his *Celtic Film Company*, was recently discovered in Bray. Carefully restored, the camera is now one of a number of interesting audiovisual exhibits on display at the town's new Heritage Centre. The most entertaining item on display is a 'mutoscope', replete with some two and a half thousand picture cards of Charlie Chaplin. This may be cranked manually to give the appearance of watching a short movie. It was manufactured by the International Mutoscope Reel Company of New York and is perhaps the only exhibit of its kind in Ireland.

Power's films included *Willie Scouts While Jessie Pouts* but he is remembered principally for having directed *Rosaleen Dhu* in 1918. This was a full-length romantic feature which was popular at the time. Power died when thrown from a horse at Leopardstown during the shooting of his next film. His cameraman on *Rosaleen Dhu* was reputedly blind, using his sensitive hands to control the speed.

During World War II, Laurence Olivier shot the battle-scenes for *Henry V* at Powerscourt, deploying soldiers of the neutral Irish army as extras. Ardmore Studios was founded in 1958 and has survived on a mixed diet of Irish and international productions which on many occasions have used the Bray area for locations. All four Irish Oscar winners are named.

Recently Neil Jordan recreated 'Bloody Sunday of 1920' at the Carlisle Grounds as part of his film about Michael Collins. The plot of Jordan's latest book, *Sunrise with sea monster* (London, 1994), is mainly located in Bray.

Sources: Anthony Slide, *The cinema and Ireland*, (North Carolina, 1988), p.18; K. Rockett, L. Gibbons and J. Hill, *Cinema and Ireland* (London, 1988), p. 48 n.39; 'Locations' in *MTM Ardmore*, i, no. 2 (March, 1989); Liam O'Leary, 'William J. Power: A Bray film pioneer' in *Ardmore Ireland.*, i, no. 1 (April/May 1990), pp. 26-28; *Bray People*, 26 March 1993, p. 7. The serial number of the Gaumont Camera is 180.

Nowhere to run: In AD 1021 Sigtryggar, son of Oafr, Scandanavian king of Dublin, was defeated at the Viking settlement of Delgany, Co. Wicklow, by Augaire mac Dunlaing. king of Leinster.

Nugget: For Uchadan and gold see Geraldine Stout, 'Wicklow's prehistoric landscape' in *Wicklow: history and society*, pp. 12-13.

Song of the streets and of the woods: In 1865 Victor Hugo wrote the preface which I have translated here and to which I add a rejoinder (Victor Hugo, *Les chansons des rues et des bois* (Editions Gallimard, 1982), p. 34).

Foundations: Saint Andrew's and Newcourt Schools share facilities on a site behind Bray Head. St. Andrew's is a free, co-educational, primary school, managed jointly by the Church of Ireland and the Presbyterian and Methodist churches and attended by Bah'ais and Catholics amongst others. There are only two such tripartite Christian schools in Ireland. Most schools are controlled by a single denomination. Newcourt is a special school. Mary Robinson was sworn in as the president of the Republic of Ireland on 3 December 1990. 'Sir' is Mr Peter McCrodden, B. A., H. Dip. Ed., headmaster of St Andrew's, who has written a dissertation on the management of learning difficulties and integrated education.

Easter Saturday: The 'Holy Year' cross on Bray Head was unveiled in September 1950. It is thirty feet high, with an arm span of twelve feet and it was 'reckoned it will last at least seventy years' from 1950. According to the *Wicklow People*, 5,000 parishioners climbed up for the ceremony, most following behind the boys of St Brighid's Youth Movement and pipe band. The photograph published with the report shows only about one hundred gathered at the cross. The cross was the project of Canon Moriarty, parish priest of Bray, who won for it 'unanimous and enthusiastic approval' from the urban council. Canon Moriarty claimed to be the first priest born in Wicklow Town. In a short address to those who climbed up for the unveiling he said that 'the erection of the cross would bring blessings on the people of Bray and County Wicklow and it would teach them the lesson of greater love and charity towards their fellow men'. The rosary was recited. One of the Quinn family of Bray Head is Fergal Quinn of *Superquinn* (*Wicklow People*, 16, 23 & 30 Sept. 1950; Jason Forde, *A* [video] *portrait of Bray* (Bray, 1994). For the last lines of the poem see Joyce, *Portrait of the Artists*, p.141).

An barr buidhe: 'Buí' (or 'buidhe') is an Irish word for 'yellow', 'buíochas' for 'gratitude'. 'Barr' is 'top' or 'crop'. The title of this poem is taken from a line by the sixteenth century poet, Laoisioch Mac an Bhaird, scolding someone who adopted fashions of the Tudor conquerors: 'Ní modh leatsa an barr buidhe: *You* think a shock of yellow hair unfashionable'. The final verses in Irish are from 'An Bonnán Buí (The Yellow Bittern)' by Cahal Buí Mac Giolla Ghunna (c.1680-1756), translated by Thomas Kinsella as '[Yellow] Bittern, I'm sorry to see you stretched with your bones decayed and eaten away' (Seán O Tuama and Thomas Kinsella, *An Duanaire 1600-1900: poems of the dispossessed* (Portlasoise, 1981), pp. 132-33; Seán MacReamoinn (ed.), *The pleasures of Gaelic poetry* (London, 1982), p. 204).

Easter Sunday: Eugene Curry ('Ordnance survey letters') refers in 1838 to a 'well in a hollow on the brink of the cliff and under the very nose of Bray Head'. He writes that some called it the Church Well, but older people called it Patrick's Well. He records a 'faint tradition' that St Patrick made this spring but found that the salt spray sometimes reached it and, therefore, opened another to the west of the church. Canon Scott (*Stones of Bray* , p.43) notes that the spring issued at the foot of the cliff just at the edge of the shingle in Naylor's Cove. The bank at this point has been re-inforced by large, ugly, cement blocks, dated 1930.

Little is known about the ruined church of Raheenaclig on the side of Bray Head. The oak in pre-Christian Ireland was a sacred tree. There are oak trees all around Raheenaclig. Given the fact that the chapel surmounts a rath it is possible that the site was in use since ancient times.

'Raheenaclig' (various spellings) is thought to be from the Irish 'Raithin' for 'Little rath' and 'clog' for a bell or round hill. The chapel appears to date from the 1200s or earlier. Curry refers to a second window remaining in 1838 but since lost. He seems to mistake his compass points.

In 1530 Raheenaclig was an Augustinian chapel, endowed by the Archbolds, who then held the Manor of Bray. At the time of the Down survey, James Archbold appears to have held a house at 'Rahanacligge' but no trace of this survives, although Curry found the sites of two smaller buildings in 1838 (Scott, *Stones of Bray*, pp.149, 181-82, 203 citing Archbishop Alan's 'Repertorium Viride'; Price, *Place-names*, pp. 332-33).

It is sometimes said that the chapel was associated with St Brendan or St Michael. But is there any possibility that 'clog' is somehow a reference to St Colum, as in the family name of the MacGiollamocholmógs who once controlled the territory around Bray Head?

Many biblical manuscripts, known collectively as the Dead Sea Scrolls, were found in caves at Qumran, east of Jerusalem, between 1947 and 1956. The first find was by a Bedouin shepherd boy, Muhammad adh-Dhib. The scrolls may help to give us a clearer picture of Jesus and his times but it has been alleged that church authorities have been responsible for the failure to publish the text of many of the manuscripts, fearing their effect on some traditional teachings. See, for example, Michael Baigent and Richard Leigh, *The Dead Sea Scrolls deception* (London, 1991).

One of the oldest churches in Paris, St Julien-le-Pauvre, was first mentioned in historical documents by Gregory of Tours about AD 580. It was rebuilt in Gothic style by monks at the end of the twelfth century. Since 1953 it has been used by Orthodox Catholics, whose spiritual leader is the patriarch of Antioch, Alexandria and Jerusalem. The French phrases are from the current Orthodox liturgy. Shortly after completing this poem I discovered that St Patrick used regularly to encourage Irish Christians to invoke the Kyrie ('Lord have mercy'/'Seigneur ayez pitié'). Thus, 'in order to be Christians like the Romans...let every church which follows me chant Kyrie Eleison, Christe Eleison' (A. B. E. Hood (ed.), *St Patrick: his writings and Muirchú's 'Life'* (London and Chichester, 1978), p. 39, p. 60).

The secret tunnel: For the suggestion of a secret tunnel from Raheenaclig Church to Smuggler's Cave see Weston St John Joyce, *The neighbourhood of Dublin* (Dublin, 1912), pp. 85-86; The friends of historic Rathdown, *Ancient Rathdown and Saint Crispin's Cell*, p.37.

Prague spring: 'Praha' is what Czechs call Prague. The old stone Karluv Most (Charles Bridge) spans the River Vltava, connecting the Stare Mesto (Old Town) with the Mala Strana (Little Quarter). On the bridge stands a bronze crucifix, which since 1696 has borne a Hebrew inscription meaning, 'Holy, Holy, Holy Lord'. During 1993 this author worked for a short period at Charles University. It is said to be the second oldest European university.

The statue of Jan Hus, a reforming preacher executed in 1415, is a focus for patriotic sentiment. The 'narodni obrozeni' was a national revival movement which led to the foundation of the First Republic in 1918. It is thought that the biggest statue of Stalin in central Europe was erected in Prague.

The 'Good King Wenceslas' of the carol is based loosely on Duke Vaclav, whose equestrian statue is at the top of Vaclavske Namesti (Wenceslas Square). A celibate Christian, he became too friendly with the Germans for the liking of his compatriots and was stabbed to death by his brother two days after the feast of St Stephen in AD 929. In the same square as the statue is the balcony from which in 1968 Alexander Dubcek defied the forces of the USSR and in which an eternal flame burns for Jan Palach, the young student who immolated himself in protest at the Soviet invasion. Now McDonald's is one of a number of western companies which have acquired and transformed the old buildings in the square. *Kiss FM* is Prague's most popular music radio station. It is run by the Dublin radio station, *Classic Hits 98FM*, and is regarded by some Czechs as symptomatic of malign capitalist influences from abroad.

The Good Soldier Svejk was written by Jaroslav Hasek. The Koruna or crown is Czech currency. The Baroque church of St Nicholas (sv Mikulas) is in Mala Strana. The Hrad, or Prague Castle, is the residence of the Czech head of state and dominates the city from a hill. 'Havel na Hrad' or '[Vaclav] Havel to the Castle' was a popular election slogan in December 1989.

Monster hotel: The International Hotel, Bray, was built during 1861 and 1862. Described in the *Dublin Builder* (1 Feb. 1861, p. 412 and 1 June 1862, p. 138) as a 'monster hotel' and 'mammoth building', the International was popular until destroyed by fire in the 1970s. It and Breslin's, just over the railway and also destroyed by fire, completed the fine streetscape of Quinsborough Road. Both appear in the damaged Lawrence photograph reproduced here. For a humorous story of how one donkey, meant for giving rides on the esplanade, ran off with Stanislaus Joyce and did not stop until the trough at the town hall was reached see *My Brother's Keeper*, pp. 35-36. The International is now the site of a bowling alley and Breslin's is a pub and offices, neither of the new buildings having as much to commend themselves architecturally as had their predecessors. My parents spent the first night of their honeymoon in the Esplanade Hotel on the seafront.

And the red light: Niall Quinn, author and merchant seaman, has written a number of books, including *Voyavic and other stories* (1980, US edition as *Brigitte and other stories* (1981)), *Stolen Air* (1988) and *Welcome To Gomorrah* (1994). The working title of the latter had been 'And the Red Light', which is a reference to some lines in an old Blues song: 'When the train left the station, It had two lights on behind; The blue one was my blues, And the red light was my mind'. Quinn won the first Brendan Behan Memorial Fellowship, only to find himself penniless at an American university when the promised support did not materialise (See *Books Ireland* (November, 1994), pp 276-7 and *Welcome to Gomorrah*, passim).

Welcome to the world: This writer once made a documentary for RTE Radio 1 which involved his flying to New York in the cockpit of a Jumbo jet. He has visited and worked in that city on a number of occasions.

Coyote/Gondola: 'Tunnel' and 'Sulphur' mountains are at Banff, Alberta. The 'Panoramic Summit' restaurant is said to be Canada's highest!

The cold facts: The Columbia Icefield (325 sq. km.) is the largest body of ice in the Rocky Mountains, lying close to the border between British Columbia and Alberta, in Jasper National Park, Canada.

Seattle rattle: 'Interstate no. 5' is the main highway south through the north-western United States. The 'Hammering Man' ('dark man on First Avenue') is a tall steel silhouette figure with anvil and moving hammer, which stands outside the Seattle Art Museum. It was made in 1992 by Jonathan Borofsky. Bertolucci's *Little Buddha* was filmed partly in Seattle. Kurt Cobain, the famous lead singer with Seattle's 'Nirvana' rock group, commited suicide in 1994. The area has also been associated with the singer Bing Crosby and with the manufacture of Boeing jets.

Grist to whose mill: The Martello tower which formerly stood on the seafront may be seen clearly in the sketch by Packer reproduced on the cover of this book and in a painting of Bray by Erskine Nicol in the National Gallery of Ireland. For Naylor see Snowy Gallagher, 'Sam Naylor: a Bray fisherman' in *Bray Historical Record*, no.vi (1993). Fiddler's Bridge is said to be so called because a blind fiddler used to come from Cork each summer and busk there for tourists.

Brunel's folly: Isambard Kingdom Brunel was the leading British engineer of his day. However, his line around Bray Head had to be restructured a number of times due to landslips and to structural weaknesses. Wooden viaducts which he erected, similar to those which he engineered in the West Country of England, proved unsuccessful and were abandoned. Lord Meath is said to have refused to countenance the railway passing near his house on the land side of Bray Head and to have insisted that it follow its present precarious path. At one point, some unkind persons dubbed the project 'Brunel's folly' (K. A. Murray, 'Bray, Brunel and all that' in *Ir. Railway Record Soc. Jn.*, v, no. 26 (Spring, 1960); Murray, 'Bray Head' in *Ir. Railway Record Soc. Jn.*, xiv, no. 82 (June, 1980); Murray, 'The coming of the railway' in *The Book of Bray*, pp. 78-85).

Gerald: The poem refers to an encounter which occurred on 5 Jan. 1995. On 7 Aug. 1867 a train from Enniscorthy to Dublin was derailed as it crossed a wooden viaduct on Bray Head in the area from Brabazon Corner to 'Ram's Scalp'. Fortunately, it fell on the landside as the loss would have been greater had it gone down into the sea. At least two people were killed and twenty-three were seriously injured and removed with great difficulty to the Rathdown Union. Following an investigation two railway workers were dismissed, it being concluded that the accident was caused by negligence in the laying of tracks (Kevin A. Murray, 'Bray Head' in *Ir. Railway Record Soc. Jn.*, xiv, no. 82 (June, 1980), pp. 77, 80-81).

Dún Brea: This poem reworks an ancient mythological account of the origin of the place-name 'Dún Brea', which was very possibly the earliest name for the Bray area (see above). The account was recorded nearly one thousand years ago in the tract known as the 'Dindshenchas', which is found in the Book of Lecan and elsewhere. I have used the translations of both Curry and Gwynn. The 'dún' fort is associated with the Early Iron Age, hence the reference to cooking cauldrons. Brea is said to have 'instituted...the roofed hunting-booth of osier', hence the mention of a 'hide' or blind (Curry, 'Ordnance survey letters', pp. 28-29, 36; Edward Gwynn (ed.), 'The metrical Dindshenchas, part III' in *R.I.A.Todd lecture series, x* (Dublin, 1913), pp. 110-13. See also pp. 146-47 above).

There was a day: This poem is based on an old Irish story of rebirth, as it has come down in a version composed almost one thousand years ago. In this occurs one of the earliest references to Bray, or Dún Brea as the place is believed to have been known previously. Until the coming of St Patrick I have followed closely the version of the story translated into English by Kuno Meyer. For the later period, which I have invented, I have also incorporated some phrases from the old tale (For Kuno Meyer, 'Tuan mac Cairill's story to Finnen of Moville' see Alfred Nutt, *The Celtic doctrine of re-birth, with appendices* (London, 1897), pp. 76-82, 289-301).

There was an ancient oratory or place of penance in the Bray area, possibly at the later site of St Paul's Church or at Oldcourt or Raheenaclig (Scott, *Stones of Bray*, pp. 201-02; Price, *Place-names v*, 334-35).

Sir Walter de Ridelesford built a Norman castle at Bray but it had been completely destroyed by the nineteenth century. The wheel of its mill was still in place until quite recently and the millrace was only filled in during the 1990s. For a rambling poetic romance about de Ridelesford's castle, often confused with the smaller castle which survived across the river in Little Bray until the *Superquinn* shopping centre was built, see 'The wraith of de Riddlesford's Castle' in George Armstrong, *Stories of Wicklow* (London, 1892), pp. 292-351.